PRAISE FOR *PRACTICE PERFECT*

"The critical difference between 'good-enough' and exemplary is not talent or desire. It's practice. Deliberate practice. That's why *Practice Perfect* is such an immensely important book. It's the first to provide evidence-based rules, rich examples, and detailed techniques on how to design and conduct practice routines. If you want to improve your own—or someone else's—performance, you've got to read this book. The authors have given everyone a great gift in *Practice Perfect.* They've handed over the key that unlocks excellence. Take that key and use it. Now."

—Jim Kouzes, coauthor of the bestselling *The Leadership Challenge*;
Dean's Executive Fellow of Leadership, Leavey School of Business,
Santa Clara University

"Doug Lemov has done it again. In *Practice Perfect*, one of America's best teachers widens his focus to help all of us move ever closer to mastery. If you are interested in getting better at anything (or helping someone else get better), then this book, with its excellent collection of techniques and tools, should be your field guide."

—Daniel H. Pink, author of *Drive* and *A Whole New Mind*

"A timely, winning, and approachable proposition! The pursuit of improvement through the development of a disciplined approach to practice is an essential element to success in all your pursuits."

—Douglas R. Conant, former president, chief executive officer,
and director of Campbell Soup Company; *New York Times*
Best Selling Author of *TouchPoints*; ASTD 2012 Champion
of Workplace Learning and Performance

"There are no shortcuts to success, whether it be in education, sports, or business. The authors of *Practice Perfect* provide a clear-cut, commonsense blueprint for what we all need to know to create practice habits that ensure permanent, sustainable results. I especially hope all aspiring teachers read this book. Transforming our public schools isn't going to be easy, but it can be done through hard work and the right kind of practice—the kind taught explicitly in this book."

—Michael D. Eisner, former chairman and chief executive officer,
Walt Disney Company; founder, The Tornante Company;
cofounder, The Eisner Foundation

"*Practice Perfect* will provide a recipe for organizations that are committed to their people—to helping them grow and get better in simple but powerful—and perhaps overlooked—ways. *Practice Perfect* will create the conditions I believe necessary to equip schools, school leaders, and teachers with the tools essential for student success."

—Jean-Claude Brizard, chief executive officer, Chicago Public Schools

"Just like *Teach Like a Champion, Practice Perfect* is a treasure trove full of perfectly polished, just the right size 'gems.' I couldn't read it fast enough. I wanted to quickly pick up each of the ideas the three authors crafted and figure out how to bring the practices into my own work. Building on the work of the Heath brothers, Atul Gawande, Daniel Coyle, Marcus Buckingham, Daniel Willingham, and others, the authors take a classic problem—the gap between knowing what to do and actually doing it—and provide forty-two wise and practical 'rules' to close that gap. Each rule is grounded in a story and related in a familiar tone, making it a fast and fun, and often even funny, read. Each of the rules is a concrete, actionable means to help ourselves and those we are coaching or managing to do the very thing it is we want to do but have not figured out how to do yet."

—Heather Kirkpatrick, vice president of education, Aspire Public Schools

"*Practice Perfect* sets a new bar for how to practice and will be a resource that I will return to time and again. The way that I will lead practice won't only be better on Monday, but every day."

—Brent Maddin, Ed.D., provost, Relay Graduate School of Education

"It's become conventional wisdom that the path to excellence—no matter whether you're a surgeon looking to hone your craft or a teacher looking for help with classroom management—is paved with hours and hours of practice. In this book the authors provide practical guidance, grounded in forty-two concrete and actionable 'rules,' for how anyone can use carefully selected, but relatively simple tasks to ensure these hours of practice lead to excellence."

—Kathleen Porter-Magee, Bernard Lee Schwartz Policy Fellow; senior director, High Quality Standards Initiative, Thomas B. Fordham Institute

Practice
Perfect

Practice Perfect

42 Rules for Getting Better at Getting Better

DOUG LEMOV
ERICA WOOLWAY
KATIE YEZZI

FOREWORD BY DAN HEATH

JOSSEY-BASS
A Wiley Imprint
www.josseybass.com

Cover image: Rob Richard
Cover design: Jeff Puda

Published by Jossey-Bass
A Wiley Imprint
One Montgomery Street, Suite 1200, San Francisco, CA 94104-4594—www.josseybass.com

Jossey-Bass books and products are available through most bookstores. To contact Jossey-Bass directly call our Customer Care Department within the U.S. at 800-956-7739, outside the U.S. at 317-572-3986, or fax 317-572-4002.

Wiley publishes in a variety of print and electronic formats and by print-on-demand. Some material included with standard print versions of this book may not be included in e-books or in print-on-demand. If this book refers to media such as a CD or DVD that is not included in the version you purchased, you may download this material at http://booksupport.wiley.com. For more information about Wiley products, visit www.wiley.com.

Library of Congress Cataloging-in-Publication Data

Lemov, Doug, 1967-
    Practice perfect : 42 rules for getting better at getting better / Doug Lemov, Erica Woolway, Katie Yezzi; foreword by Dan Heath. — 1st ed.
        p.   cm.
    Includes bibliographical references and index.
    ISBN 978-1-118-21658-3 (cloth); ISBN 978-1-118-22872-2 (ebk.);
ISBN 978-1-118-23125-8 (ebk.); ISBN 978-1-118-26619-9 (ebk.)
        1. Performance.   2. Ability.   3. Reinforcement (Psychology).   4. Success.
I. Woolway, Erica, 1979-   II. Yezzi, Katie, 1980-   III. Title.
BF481.L45 2012
650.1—dc23

                                                                                    2012026295

Printed in the United States of America
FIRST EDITION
HB Printing   10   9   8   7   6   5   4   3   2   1

CONTENTS

FOREWORD

In the summer of 2011, my wife, my parents, and I took a tour of a whisky distillery in Scotland. The tour guide seemed almost catatonically bored. At each stop, she'd recite a memorized script and then ask, "Are there any questions?" but of course there weren't, because that would mean we'd been listening. And what I remember most about the tour—other than wishing we could skip ahead to the tasting—was that I spent most of my time thinking about Chris Rock.

I'd been reading a book (*Little Bets* by Peter Sims) that described Rock's process in developing new material for his standup act. In preparing for one tour, Rock made between 40 and 50 appearances at a small club in New Brunswick, New Jersey. He'd show up, carrying a yellow legal pad with his ideas scribbled on it, and start experimenting with new bits. Sims writes, "He watches the audience intently, noticing heads nodding, shifting body language, or attentive pauses, all clues as to where good ideas might reside. In sets that run around forty-five minutes, most of the jokes fall flat."

But with time, he digs out the material that works. The jokes get sharper and the transitions get tighter and the delivery gets smoother. (So if you've ever cracked up at one of Rock's lines—"I live in a neighborhood so bad you can get shot while getting shot"—then you might have New Jersey to thank.)

By the time Rock performs the routine for an HBO special, or in an appearance on David Letterman, he has long since mastered the material. Perfected it. And, as a result, he'll give the illusion of effortlessness: *Chris Rock is such a funny guy.*

A few months after the whisky tour, I was giving a speech, and I caught myself telling a story the same rote way I'd told it a dozen times before. And a nasty thought struck: *I am the whisky tour guide.* (Thankfully, I stopped short of verbalizing this thought, thus avoiding what could have been a deeply confusing moment.)

In life, we'll face this choice again and again: to be the whisky tour guide or to be Chris Rock. Will we be content to cruise along on autopilot or will we scramble and suffer to get better? Will we plod or will we practice? This book is a guidebook for anyone willing to make the latter choice.

There are many full-stop moments in the pages that follow—ideas so interesting that you can't help but pause for a second and consider them. One of those ideas is that practice doesn't make perfect, *practice makes permanent.* For example, you have been shampooing your hair for decades and yet *you are not getting any better at it.* (As a matter of fact, you will likely die never knowing whether there was a better shampooing technique.) The mere fact of doing something repeatedly does not help us improve.

What we need is practice—real practice, not mere repetition. As Michael Jordan said, "You can practice shooting eight hours a day, but if your technique is wrong, then all you become is very good at shooting the wrong way." Practice makes permanent.

As kids, we were constantly practicing something: shooting a basketball, playing the piano, learning some Spanish. Those practices could be a drag—it's the rare athlete who can't wait for wind sprints—but because they were thoughtfully designed, they came with a wonderful payoff: the certainty of improvement. From week to week, we couldn't help but get better.

How did practice get squeezed out of our lives? Certainly the need hasn't disappeared—practice is as critical for our performance in the office as it was for the playing field and the concert hall. There's a long list of skills we'd all be wise to hone: *How to run a meeting that doesn't drag on. How to listen (really listen) to your spouse. How to get through a stressful commute without barking out profanities.*

The enemies of practice are pride and fear and self-satisfaction. To practice requires humility. It forces us to admit that we don't know everything. It forces us to submit to feedback from people who can teach us. But surely practice isn't a sign of weakness—after all, some of the people most famously disciplined about practice are Michael Jordan, Jerry Rice, Roger Federer, Mia Hamm, and Tiger Woods. To practice isn't to declare, *I'm bad.* To practice is to declare, *I can be better.*

And of course we're all practicing *something* every day. Twenty-four hours of daily practice. We're practicing the way we interact with our kids and the way we collaborate with our colleagues. The question is: Are we getting better? Are we plodding or are we practicing?

The fact that you bought this book suggests you're a Practicer. If so, you've chosen the right handbook.

Prepare to get better at getting better.

—Dan Heath, *senior fellow at Duke University's CASE center; coauthor of* Made to Stick *and* Switch

For our children. We wish them a world of possibilities.

PREFACE: WHY PRACTICE? WHY NOW?

The three of us are first and foremost teachers. And though this book is for readers in a wide variety of fields, it began some time ago as a book for and about teachers. Still, if you are a parent or a manager or a coach or a mentor or a leader in your organization, you'd have a hard time convincing us you weren't a teacher anyway, so perhaps the book was always destined to become something broader. But in the end, because we are teachers first and foremost, this book tends to see the world from an educator's perspective.

So forgive us if we begin by saying something strange about teaching, which is that we are optimistic—humble, but optimistic. We are optimistic not only because we still believe that the greatest, most gratifying work in the world is teaching someone how to factor a quadratic equation, field a ground ball, run a meeting, read a nineteenth-century novel, or examine an elderly patient with insight and compassion. We are also optimistic because we think that the teaching profession is on the brink of greatness. Teachers around the country feel attacked and cornered in a climate marked, they say, by the overlap of political turmoil and austerity budgets. But when those temporary aberrations fade, we will be left with a series of creative tensions that just may reshape the profession, giving it for the first time a clear way to study and learn from itself, and providing it the tools to get better in ways we'd never before considered. This will happen not just through practice but also in the use of data and analytical tools to find out and capitalize on what teachers do best—"Bright Spots," in the words of Chip and Dan Heath, who wrote the Foreword to this volume and whose work inspires us and so many others.

We are also humble, though, because we have made many mistakes—several of them public and some more embarrassing than others—in learning what we think can be a small part of the equation that reframes teaching. We are humbled because we believe humility—constantly facing the likelihood that our work could and should have been better—to be the way to do our work in this world. We are humbled so much that we almost didn't dare write this book. And yet we did, because we think it can help, within the teaching profession and well beyond.

This book is about what the three of us—Doug, Erica, and Katie—learned in responding to the struggle for talent in one very important sector of the economy, public education, and in attacking one very critical social problem, the achievement gap between children of privilege and children of poverty. But it's also about what this experience led us to observe about developing talent in other sectors of our lives and other sectors of society. So while we believe this book has important lessons for the field of education specifically, and while we often write about examples from our work in schools and in training teachers, we believe it is also relevant to a wide range of organizations and people who want to get better, who must get better. We also think this book is applicable beyond education because we have each gone through the process of applying what we've learned in the hothouse of our professional lives to the world of our personal lives. Having redesigned the trainings we provide for teachers over and over to wring incremental improvement, we constantly see the issues we faced in that struggle as we try to raise our own children to be caring and positive as people and skilled as mathematicians and musicians and soccer players. We see the issues as we try to develop our own skills at skiing and home repair, at knitting, managing people, and most recently, at writing books. The first step is getting better *at* getting better.

In these cases we see the role that a humble and overlooked servant could play in spinning straw into gold. That servant is the underestimated concept of *practice.* Generally seen as mundane and humdrum, poorly used and much maligned, or too familiar to be interesting, practice is often considered unworthy of deep, sustained reflection and precise engineering.

We had each separately been working for years on how to help people get better at teaching: Doug as a teacher and school leader, who later delved into his study of champion teachers that would become the highly successful and instructive text, *Teach Like a Champion*; Erica as a teacher, grade team chair, and then founding dean of students, who came to the techniques in *Teach Like a Champion* as a young school leader hungry for a common language to use with developing teachers; and Katie, who came to the team having spent 15 years as a teacher, principal, and consultant to charter schools. She found the collection of techniques in the "Taxonomy" (as it was known before the book's publication) a revelation: it made outstanding teaching replicable. In the fall of 2008 Erica and Katie joined Doug's team to develop ways to train other school leaders in these techniques. The techniques in *Teach Like a Champion* were aimed at transforming the lives of all teachers and students, whether they were in district schools, private schools, or charter schools. But what was surprising was how many people—coaches, parents, tutors, medical faculty, and professors of higher education—saw other applications. So when we looked closer at practice, we looked for broader applications and drew from fields that were much more developed on the topic of practice than teaching.

Along the way, at the recommendation of our colleague Paul Bambrick-Santoyo, we read Daniel Coyle's *The Talent Code* about various hotbeds of talent throughout the world that have shown us the key elements that lead to talent development. We took away many useful lessons from this book, not the least of which was the central role of practice in the development of talent. We read Gladwell, Gawande, Dweck, and Willingham, trying to better understand how we could take the techniques of champion teachers and develop them in others. We were completely convinced by, and perhaps obsessed with, practice, but we lacked a practice manual. So we revised our practice activities, going on instinct and searching for what worked. Our conversations always came back to practice: What does effective practice look like? What separates true practice from repetition or performance? And what were the key design principles to ensure that practice truly made performance better? And so we arrived at the work before you: a collection of 42 rules to shape and improve how you use practice to get better.

We begin these rules by asking you to rethink your preconceived notions about practice. We address this first because these notions lay the foundation for practice. In the next three chapters we present practical rules for how to set up practice and use the power of modeling and feedback. In the fifth and sixth chapters we look at how to build and maintain a team that embraces practice and leverages its power. Success—for individuals, for organizations, for communities, even for nations—is the struggle for talent. More specifically, it is the struggle to attract talent and the struggle to develop talent, to make people better. Though this has perhaps always been true, the lines of this struggle have never been as starkly drawn as they are today, when local competition is global, when talent is more urgently required throughout every seat in an organization, and where specialization yields higher standards for individual effectiveness. The rules in this book will assist you in developing talent in a highly competitive world, and help you get better at getting better—one practice at a time.

Practice Perfect

THE POWER OF PRACTICE

Everybody has the will to win;
few people have the will to prepare to win.
—BOBBY KNIGHT

It's a funny thing. The more I practice the luckier I get.
—ARNOLD PALMER

John Wooden is a legend. The coach of UCLA's basketball team for 27 years, he was anointed "Greatest Coach of the 20th Century" by ESPN and the greatest coach ever—in any sport—by the *Sporting News*. Wooden led his teams to ten national championships in 12 years, won 88 consecutive games, and achieved the highest winning percentage (.813) of any coach in NCAA basketball history—all while building an enduring reputation for developing the character of his players at least as much as their skill. It's not surprising that in the decades since Wooden retired, his influence has spread far beyond the basketball court. Books by and about Wooden apply his insights to life, learning, and business as much as to basketball.

Regardless of any interest in sports, people study Wooden's methods for the alchemy that turns struggle into triumph. And yet the great majority of students of his work fail to replicate

Wooden-like results. Why? Our answer, based on what we—Doug, Erica, and Katie—discovered in our efforts to help promising teachers become great teachers, is that most people fail to realize the power of the one thing that is arguably the secret of Wooden's success: old-fashioned practice, efficiently run, well-planned, and intentionally executed.

If you were to ask Wooden what made his teams so successful, he would likely describe a series of unacknowledged moments in otherwise empty gymnasiums: his players practicing shooting without a basketball, say. Or perhaps he'd describe his evenings in his office scripting the next day's practice, noting where the racks of basketballs should be placed so time was never wasted looking for a ball. John Wooden doted on practice to a degree that was legendary. He began—surely to much eye rolling—by practicing things that every other coach would have considered unworthy, if they'd have considered them at all: how to put on socks and sneakers, for example.[1] He timed his practices to the minute, husbanding every second to ensure its precise and careful allocation. He kept a record of every practice on note cards, which he filed away for future reference: what worked; what didn't; how to do it better next time. Unlike many coaches, he focused not on scrimmaging—playing in a way that *replicated* the game—but on drilling, that is playing in ways that intentionally *distorted* the game to emphasize and isolate specific concepts and skills. He followed a logical progression, often starting his instruction on topics like shooting by having players work without the ball and building to increasingly challenging applications. He repeated drills until his players achieved mastery and then automaticity, even if it meant not drilling on more sophisticated topics. At the point where other coaches might decide their teams had learned a skill, Wooden's teams were just beginning their work. And he always insisted that his players practiced doing it—whatever "it" was—right.

Though we remember him for the championships, what ultimately made Wooden great was practice. Every iteration of teaching and explaining and executing again and again was a tiny bit better than anyone else's. The culture in which those drills took place—what players were thinking as they stood in lines—was a little bit more humble, selfless, relentless. The compounded effect of these tiny differences was a dynasty.

Author and sportswriter Daniel Coyle's book *The Talent Code* is just one of several recent efforts to understand the tradition of intentional practice that Wooden helped establish. In the book, Coyle describes how the compounded effect of better practice accounts for the rise of seemingly inexplicable "hot spots" of talent around the globe. What seems like talent, it turns out, is often better practice habits in disguise. How could it be, for example, that a single tennis club in a freezing climate—a club Coyle describes as "rundown" and with just one indoor court—has, since its founding, produced more top-20 women players than all of the tennis clubs in the United States put together?

The answer is Larisa Preobrazhenskaya, the gray-haired, track-suit-wearing majordomo whose players follow the adage that practice makes permanent—that if practice drives actions into muscle memory, it's better to do it slow and right than fast and not quite right. Like John Wooden, she practices fewer things better, and with diligence. She is unapologetic about asking her athletes to imitate others, an approach that many coaches too often dismiss as demeaning. Via these simple obsessions, Coyle tells us, Preobrazhenskaya has almost single-handedly changed Russia's perception of itself. The initial success of her players caused an explosion of interest in tennis in Russia that fed the practice mill with aspiring players and produced success on such a massive scale that it appeared to be a statistical impossibility. Today Russia sees itself as a tennis nation made of players who believe they can do just about anything.

Again and again Coyle shows that the aggregation of seemingly trivial improvements in practice can create otherwise inexplicable densities of talent sufficient to change a society and its conception of what is possible. Brazil's passion for soccer makes it an international power, but its passion for *futsal*, a soccer derivative featuring small-sided games in an enclosed space using a less elastic ball, yields as many as six times the touches per hour for a developing Brazilian player, Coyle points out, than for a similar player in some other nation. The game's space limitations reward skills learned to speedy automaticity. "Commentators love to talk about how 'creative' Brazilian players are—but that's not quite right. The truth is, they've been practicing that creativity for their entire lives," writes Coyle. The humble details of their practice separate Brazil from every other soccer-obsessed nation on Earth.

For its part, the United States remains a competition-loving culture. We love the heroic upset, the last hurrah of the aging veteran, the final ticking seconds as the game comes down to the wire. We watch games and follow teams and players, sometimes to the point of obsession (especially if our kids are playing), but if we really wanted to see greatness—to cheer for it and understand what made it happen—we'd spend our time watching practices instead. We would pay a lot more attention to how drills were designed, to a culture of humility and perseverance among the players, to whether there was enough practice, or indeed—as we will soon discover—whether there was any practicing at all.

Imagine for a moment what it would be like if we could manufacture "hot spots" like the one Coyle describes among Russian tennis players. Imagine if we could cause a spike in performance sufficient to change a society's perception of what it is possible to achieve by and for its people. Imagine if we could apply it not just to our own soccer and tennis programs but also to things far more important than sports: to running better hospitals and schools, to a thousand endeavors across the economy where entrepreneurs and managers create value for the people who rely on and benefit from their products and services.

This book is not really about sports, then, though we are confident that you will be able to apply its conclusions in that setting if *you* are all about basketball or soccer or skiing. Our purpose in writing this book is to engage the dream of "better," both in fields where participants know they should practice, but could do it more effectively, and also in endeavors where most people do not yet recognize the transformative power of practice. Deliberately engineered and designed, practice can revolutionize our most important endeavors; in that, we speak from at least a bit of experience.

■ ■ ■

Our own journey to understanding the power of practice began with an ad hoc study of great teachers in our nation's high-poverty public schools: work outlined in Doug's book *Teach Like a Champion*. This study revealed that positive outliers—teachers who were anomalously and sometimes breathtakingly successful in the face of adversity—were a lot like John Wooden. They were the most likely to focus on small and seemingly mundane aspects of their daily work.

Great teachers obsessed on things like how efficiently they used time in the classroom. They fought a running battle for seconds and minutes by paying careful attention to how (and how quickly) their students lined up or passed out papers. They perseverated on the words they used to explain a concept. This struck us as ironic. The teachers whose students had best mastered the higher order, the abstract, and the rigorous—a deep reading of symbolism in *Lord of the Flies,* or reliably solving equations with two unknowns—were those teachers most likely to obsess on things that others thought unworthy of attention. There was more to it than that, obviously. Great teachers did more than obsess on the efficiency of their classroom—their questions were artful; their assignments, demanding—but there was a clear tendency among positive outliers to see the power of the humdrum, the everyday. Think here of John Wooden on the first day of practice, teaching his players to put their socks on correctly. So many of the great teachers, we realized, also had a socks-first mentality. We glimpsed their excellence and wanted to help everyone get a piece of it. So we set out to show teachers in our schools how to get better by studying the ways great teachers taught. In the process, we learned a lot about practice, what makes it work and what makes it not work very well. One of the first things we noticed was something we now call the "get it/do it gap."

During our first workshops we would show teachers one short video clip after another of superstar colleagues demonstrating a particular technique. We would analyze and discuss, and then, once our audience understood the technique in all of its nuance and variation, we went on to the next technique. Evaluations were outstanding. Participants told us they had learned useful and valuable methods to apply. But then we noticed something alarming. If we surveyed the same participants three months later, they were not quite as upbeat. They still knew what they wanted their classes to be like, but they were unable to reliably do what it took to get there. When they tried to fix one thing, something else went wrong. It was difficult to concentrate on a technique with so much else going on. Just knowing what they should be doing was not enough to make them successful.

We realized that our workshop participants, on returning to their classrooms, were trying to do the equivalent of walking onto center court at Wimbledon and learning a new style of backhand in the midst of a match. Of course they weren't winning. Tennis players know that refining your backhand means hitting hundreds or thousands of strokes before a match begins. They know that there is no way to make the thing you need in order to get better— hundreds of balls hit to your backhand at just the right height with an increasing level of difficulty—happen predictably in a match. In the match there is no way to ensure that when opportunities to apply the skill come you will have enough brain power available to think about it. Instead, you might find yourself scrambling left to right across the baseline and trying to read your opponent's reaction—the backhand itself practically an afterthought.

We realized we would have to do two things. First we would have to approach teaching like tennis. We would have to practice, right then and there in the workshops, even if it meant cutting the number of techniques we taught. Like Wooden, we'd have to do fewer things better. And we would have to shift from training teachers directly to training their coaches: principals and mentor teachers who had the power to build and orchestrate practice on a regular basis. We had to make the design of our practice an explicit part of our training. So our workshops went from being about what the techniques were to how to practice them. A single workshop, we realized, wouldn't really make people better unless it caused them to practice key skills multiple times—or to learn to practice and be able to begin a yearlong cycle of practice.

It's worth pausing for a moment here to reflect on just how strange it was to build workshops for teachers around the idea of practicing. Even though teachers, like other professionals such as doctors or lawyers, are required to continually engage in professional development, they do not engage in what people in other performance professions might call "active practice." By "performance profession" we mean any work, like sports or music or surgery, that happens in real time. If a teacher's performance during a given class is less than what she wanted, she cannot get it back. She cannot, as say a lawyer working on a contract might do, stop in the middle of her work and call someone to ask for advice. She can't give it her best shot and then, as we are doing as we write, go back and tinker and revise and have the luxury of being held accountable for a final product that reflects actions taken and reconsidered over an extended period. Teachers "go live" four or five times a day. And yet unlike other performance professionals, they don't call what they do to prepare "practice"; they call it "professional development." If we asked a roomful of teachers how often they practiced for what they did in their "game"—how often they rehearsed the questions they ask students, or the way they start class—most would look at us funny. Teachers listen, reflect, discuss, and debate, but they do not practice.

What is the effect of all this listening, reflecting, and debating? Our education system makes huge investments in helping teachers improve their knowledge and skills. A recent policy brief by the Consortium for Policy Research in Education estimated that between 3 and 6 percent of total school spending was allocated to professional development, for example.[2] Assuming the annual budget figure for public elementary and secondary schools alone is $500 billion per year, this comes out to $20–$30 billion every year. It is an investment that yields questionable results. "Teachers typically spend a few hours listening and, at best, leave with some practical tips or some useful materials. There is seldom any follow-up to the experience and subsequent in-services may address entirely different sets of topics," notes the policy brief. "On the whole, most researchers agree that local professional development programs typically have weak effects on practice because they lack focus, intensity, follow-up, and continuity." In other words, what we do to train teachers fails to make them better teachers.

Then as now, this fact was a cause for intense reflection for us. The organization where we work, a nonprofit called Uncommon Schools, runs inner-city public schools that have closed the achievement gap for poor and minority students, preparing them for college at a rate far in excess of what's previously been accomplished. While we set out to help run a system of schools that would set the standard for high performance, particularly with kids who were otherwise cut off from opportunity, we were keenly aware of the words of former British prime minister Tony Blair's chief education adviser, Sir Michael Barber, and his colleagues in their report for McKinsey on the world's best school systems: "The quality of an education system cannot exceed the quality of its teachers." While the endeavor to make schools better remains something of a national drama, it has resulted in invective, blame, and tension but little evidence of large-scale improvement. If we can't make our schools better, it must be somebody's fault: teachers, parents, some group of politicians or intriguers, perhaps even the students themselves.

Our nation's schools, having more than doubled their annual per pupil expenditures since 1970, have achieved precious little improvement against previous performances—a reduction in outcomes, in fact, if you ask the makers of the SAT. We Americans confront results that place us far below nations with the best school systems, and we wring our hands; but we can't seem to do much about it. Teachers, in your three authors' experience, are for the most part eager to learn and develop throughout their careers, but the plain fact is that we don't help them to do so. The cost, in lost opportunity, is immense.

In this sense, our work as educators is perhaps not that different from yours: you seek to execute a plan that can transform some aspect of daily life and bring immense value to you, your family, your community, and society. You seek to make a positive outlier out of your local youth soccer program, or the quality of care in your city hospital, or the way your managers develop people. If you seek to do something great, you most likely live a battle for talent—for smart and capable people who can do great things at scale.

In education, as in so many fields, the long-run battle for talent is more about growing it than attracting it. The broader struggle to change educational outcomes isn't, for the three of us, about whether we can get a limited number of game-changing teachers to teach 30 kids in our organization rather than some other organization, but about whether we can help more and more teachers perform like their game-changing peers—and reach thousands more kids. Winning is less about attracting the best parts of the talent pie than about growing the pie. The degree to which we can improve people at every skill level quickly and reliably is the measure of our success at closing the achievement gap or any of a thousand other worthy objectives.

Over time, we have been able to engineer and reengineer our training activities to improve the quality of practice within them. We are lucky in this regard in that we run workshops where we invite the best school leaders and teachers from top-performing schools to join us. These workshops are a hot house for improving the quality of our own coaching and training. The game plan is to stand up in front of a room full of a hundred or so top teachers and try to teach them about teaching. Imagine being hired to play pickup basketball in front of the LA Lakers to show them a few things that might take their game up a few notches. It had the tendency to focus our minds on every action and decision and whether it really worked. Between the mission and the setting we felt the pressure to make every minute outstanding.

Our workshops and our schools were full of people who wanted to be better teachers and were willing to work for that. We had things to teach them that could make them better. But too often we failed to do so. Here's an example: one technique that differentiated great teachers from the merely good was the way they used nonverbal interventions to correct behavior during their teaching. The idea was that using words to correct students who were in danger of becoming off task required teachers to interrupt the thread of instruction in their classroom. A teacher stopped to correct one student, and two others became distracted—a death spiral. Champion teachers solved this dilemma by using nonverbal correction. Colleen Driggs, a legendary teacher at our school in Rochester, New York, taught her students nonverbal signals to correct the three or four behaviors most likely to occur when their attention was slipping. When Colleen pointed to her eyes, it meant that students should "track the speaker"—look at the student who was talking so they would stay engaged in the conversation. When Colleen clasped her hands in front of her, it was a reminder to sit up straight. If Colleen made a brief hands-down gesture, it was a reminder for students to put their hands down while another student was talking, the idea being that if your hand remains up you are thinking about what you want to say and not really listening to your peer.

Teachers loved the video of Colleen teaching and correcting nonverbally. It seemed brilliant and obvious at the same time, and teachers were excited to try it themselves. Back at our offices we set up a sort of teaching lab to try out different practice activities. Several of us played students. We misbehaved. And while we did so, we sent a brave teacher I'll call "Jen" to the front of the room to try to teach a lesson. She did some good work, but we learned that practicing successfully was much harder than it looked. It was hard to remember to make nonverbal interventions in the moment. Jen went back to old habits under duress. Plus, we hadn't let her think through in advance how she'd handle the behaviors. Trying to decide what to do in the moment distracted her and caused her to make other mistakes. Our misbehaviors were either too frequent or too soon so that Jen never really got to the heart of her lesson. We were having such a great time channeling misbehaving students that when corrected we'd keep ratcheting things up so that there was always another thing for Jen to try to fix. She'd struggle through an interaction, think of a better response, and repeat the role play, but this time we'd model different behaviors. She never got to practice her fix. Control was always just beyond her grasp.

In the debrief Katie nailed the issue. "What Jen just did was practice failing," she said. "She practiced but she didn't really glimpse what success feels like. She's just ingrained failure even more deeply." We quickly realized one of our first rules of practice—one of the most violated yet important—which we'll discuss in the first chapter: practice should involve people practicing success, even if it means, as it did in this case, simplifying the activity. We began simplifying by making the off-task behavior predictable. Only two people were allowed to be off task. And we told Jen who they were. Now she could allocate her energy to making effective corrections. Then we realized that we needed to let Jen plan not just *any* response but the *right* response. After all, Colleen had done that in her video: she had identified the three most common behaviors beforehand and planned a gesture to correct each. So we added a preliminary activity in which the teacher got a list of typical off-task behaviors (for example, a student staring out the window; a student with her head down on the desk). Jen first had to plan what gesture she'd use to correct the student. Then she practiced making the gesture a few times. Next, she faced the class, but with the students doing the exact behaviors she'd just prepared for in a predictable order. She practiced using what she'd learned, and we made the practice more "realistic" (complex and difficult) only when she was ready for more. Eventually we added other pieces: a coach to give feedback; the requirement that Jen practice using the feedback right away by redoing the activity. We also added variables we could adapt if teachers found this activity too hard or if they were successful right away.

As we began to use this activity in workshops, we could instantly see the difference: not only in people's reactions to the workshops but in their classrooms. Teachers not only successfully implemented the techniques (we could see it clearly when we videotaped them), but they began to adapt the techniques in new and even more effective ways, which we in turn learned from and added to the trainings we offered.

Over the course of that first afternoon, the next months, and finally over several years, we honed our practice activities into tools that could help make teachers better, at scale. Somewhat unexpectedly, this made teachers happy. At first they were a bit skeptical about practicing—some of them were a lot skeptical. After all, it's awkward and makes you a bit self-conscious at first. But after a few rounds teachers could see themselves improving, both in the practice and in their classroom afterwards, and this had a powerful psychological effect. They realized that the things that happened in their classroom were within their control, that they owned what happened. Success had taught them that they could fix things, step by step. And they wanted more. Further, they enjoyed getting to work with peers in a collegial setting. Practicing together made teaching a team sport.

In the end, success and camaraderie overwhelmed any initial reluctance and embarrassment. Most teachers came to like practice and in many cases started to invent their own ways to practice. Two of our best reading teachers, Maggie Johnson and Nikki Frame, decided to get together for ten minutes a day to practice how to handle one of teaching's great problems: what to say when a student gives you an unexpected wrong answer to your question during class discussion. The solution was simple: Maggie would read questions from her lesson plan to Nikki. Nikki would give her best estimation of a wrong student answer, and Maggie would have to respond on the spot. Then they'd switch roles. At first it was hard, but they laughed and brainstormed better responses and then took it again from the top. Ten minutes a day for three, four, five weeks: at this point the difference was overwhelmingly obvious. They not only had become good at handling unexpected responses in their classes; they were confident and poised both before and after. They could relax and concentrate on the nuances of student answers and the subtleties of the text. Practice at one skill—handling the unexpected answer—had helped them to make room for improvements on a more advanced skill.

Over the years we have distilled what we've learned from dozens of situations like these—often by error, occasionally by success, almost always with the wisdom and acuity of the wise and insightful teachers in our schools and our workshops—into a set of rules, which we share in this book.

■ ■ ■

While Daniel Coyle's *The Talent Code* shows how practice has the power to transform individual performance and that individual performance in turn has the power to transform institutions, another recent book reveals how the power to transform can be applied to seemingly intractable or hopelessly complex social problems. In *Switch*, Dan and Chip Heath, a team of two brothers, one a professor of organizational behavior at Stanford, the other a senior fellow studying entrepreneurship at Duke, set out to reveal how, over and again, massive complex problems don't always require massive complex solutions. In fact identifying simple, repeatable actions that can be quickly mastered (like getting mothers to buy skim milk instead of whole) can turn the tide on seemingly resistant social phenomena (the rise of obesity). And this creates an opportunity. Many of these simple behaviors are a matter of habit. You pick up the milk you choose because it's the milk you choose. A tiny bit of practice choosing different milk leads to a massive and lasting change.

Perhaps the most compelling story in the book is of an effort to eliminate chronic malnutrition among the poorest people in Vietnam. The effort began by studying what the Heath brothers call "bright spots": the things that despite all the barriers and problems still work. They note that while many poor children grow up malnourished, many do not; so volunteers were sent to study what poor families with healthy children fed them. Turns out they ate tiny shrimp and wild field greens their mothers gathered, even though others scorned the food or walked by without knowing its value. At first other families were reluctant to follow their lead—they didn't know where to find the ingredients; they had never cooked with them before. Their habits were a barrier. But when case workers caused families to practice cooking with those ingredients, not just once but until they were familiar with it, the results were astounding. A simple change had been enough to tip the nutritional balance in the favor of thousands of families. Practiced intentionally, very simple actions could solve a massive problem and unleash a wholly unexpected power to achieve great things.

This raises an important question, which we address explicitly: Whom is practice for? Our initial response is, simply, everyone.

Everyone should practice. And it is worth looking at this notion "everyone" a lot more closely. We often start workshops with a photo of Lionel Messi—by universal acclaim the best soccer player in the world—engaged in a drill during practice.

It should be obvious that a professional soccer player practices. But in most professions outside the hypercompetitive world of professional sports and perhaps a few others—music comes to mind—we assume that practice is something that stops when you get good. Practice implies a judgment. It assumes a lack of competence. But of course this isn't true. Lionel Messi, whose work ethic is remarked on constantly, assumes that practice is a driver of his success and a key ingredient in continuing it. But there's more to the picture than the not-surprising surprise that the best still practice. It's what Messi is practicing that matters too. Perhaps we assume that for Messi practice means playing games of soccer over and over—scrimmaging, in short—so that he applies his prodigious skill to anticipate the game in all of its complexity; yet, in this photo, it is a drill he is working on, one that isolates some small aspect of his game so he can intentionally improve it. The difference between drill and scrimmage is important; it's one of the rules we discuss in the first chapter. A scrimmage replicates the game, and a drill distorts it for a purpose. Most people assume that the higher you go on the competency scale, the less drilling you need to do and the more scrimmaging. In fact, we argue, the opposite is true.

Consider the experience of surgeon and author Atul Gawande, who recently undertook a personal project, which he documents in a recent *New Yorker* article, to see how much he could improve as a surgeon. "I've been a surgeon for eight years," writes Gawande. "For the past couple of them, my performance in the operating room has reached a plateau. I'd like to think it's a good thing—I've arrived at my professional peak. But mainly it seems as if I've just stopped getting better." His logical response was to hire a coach to observe him and give him feedback. "Professional athletes use coaches to make sure they are as good as they can be," he explains, "but doctors don't. I'd paid to have a kid just out of college look at my [tennis] serve. So why did I find it inconceivable to pay someone to come into my operating room and coach me on my surgical technique?" But Gawande's decision meets with a level of skepticism and concern that reveals our collective prejudice that practice is only for the novice or the struggling practitioner. Patients and peers see the coach standing in the back of the operating theater and assume something must be amiss. Otherwise why would he be there?

In fact, using a coach to review and refine his work boosted Gawande's performance dramatically. Let's look at one small area that Gawande's coach, Dr. Osteen, zeroed in on:

> Osteen also asked me to pay more attention to my elbows. At various points during the operation, he observed, my right elbow rose to the level of my shoulder, on occasion higher. "You cannot achieve precision with your elbow in the air," he said. A surgeon's elbows should be loose and down by his sides. "When you are tempted to raise your elbow, that means you need to either move your feet"—because you're standing in the wrong position—"or choose a different instrument."

The advice was helpful, but for Gawande to use it to maximum benefit, he'd have to remember it in the midst of a complex procedure—perhaps breaking the thread of his concentration—and make the change there in the game. His first efforts to work with lowered elbows may well have corresponded to an implementation dip, the idea that as you try to incorporate a new technique your performance goes down slightly until you get good at it. Was it risky to endure that dip during surgery on a real patient?

What if Gawande and his coach had set up a drill where Gawande simulated procedures and executed them with his elbows down? Just an hour or so might have built muscle memory that could have implemented the advice of his coach effectively and at lower risk. Despite Gawande's fairly exceptional humility and desire to improve, the potential of using practice to maximize his coach's advice goes unconsidered.

Now consider how many more professions and activities are like teaching or surgery, where practice, with its potential to drive improvement—to create a culture of constant improvement—goes unharnessed. Imagine observing a meeting between a colleague who reports to you—a fellow lawyer perhaps—and a client. As you observe, you (like Gawande's coach) see some good things and some areas for improvement. What if you were working in an organization that supported coaching, feedback, and practice? What if you could give your colleague feedback after the meeting? Perhaps you'd say, "Try asking more questions. A lot more. That will help you understand the specifics of the case"—she should ask more questions so she understands the specifics of the case, for example. You engage your colleague in a discussion where she might recall the exact moments in which she could have done so. She might remember to do so on her next meeting, which would be an improvement. But she might not. And what if the meeting is critical or urgent, and she can't risk a mistake? How much better would the outcome be if you first role-played to diagnose her strengths and weaknesses and then had her practice asking more questions, until she was asking not only more but better questions to draw out the best information from the client and make the client feel supported? Finally, if you had conducted the "client meeting" practice session with not only one lawyer but several, they might have learned from each other and developed their skills at the same cost in resources and time as developing one employee. And they probably would have improved more by watching each other, learning from each other's strengths and weaknesses.

If you were able to do these things and, over time, do them outstandingly well, you would have an efficient way to develop people for the most important tasks across your organization, your team, your school, wherever you want to help yourself and others get better. You would have an advantage that might allow you to achieve—as many of the organizations that have attended our workshops have begun to do—positive, even exceptional results. You might even end up like one of the 32 franchises in the National Football League. In that hypercompetitive sector of the economy, where talent is so valuable that its allocation is regulated by a complex array of protocols—a draft, a salary cap, restricted free-agency, to name a few—coaches watch practice film at least as intently as they do game film. Consider this description from a recent *Washington Post* article profiling the approach used by Redskins head coach Mike Shanahan, an NFL legend:

> By the time [quarterback] Rex Grossman lined up . . . three video cameras manned by three cameramen rose 60 feet in the air on three massive orange lifts. . . . The play . . . appeared on a white sheet of paper with burgundy headings that listed every play to be practiced that day. Anders Beutel, the assistant equipment manager and Grossman's de facto center in such drills, held a copy of the practice script. High above the field . . . the team's video director held another copy of the script, because every play of every practice is recorded from multiple angles.

Organizations that operate in the most intense competitive settings have come to realize that practice time is the most valuable time they have, and logically this shows up in how they use video. As video has gotten exponentially easier and cheaper to produce, its use has exploded, but changes in its use are telling. In its first iteration people videotaped games in order to understand performance; in the second generation they film practices instead. The latter, they find, are more important in driving results.

■ ■ ■

In the following chapters you will find 42 rules for making your own practices the most valuable endeavors they can be. These rules were hard won: they are based not only on our years of working with teachers but on our readings and research, our own experiences and those of our children as they have strived to grow and learn, and on constant discussions about how to help people do things better. We believe in the power of small things, so you will notice that the rules sometimes go into technical detail; but we are convinced that paying attention to such detail will yield the same outstanding results for you that it has for us—perhaps even better.

In the first chapter we'll look at common assumptions about practice and as a starting point ask you to reconsider them. The second chapter will focus on design principles for running effective practices. The third looks at the role modeling can play in increasing the effectiveness of practice sessions, and the fourth explores the important role of feedback. The fifth chapter considers practice as a social activity and therefore one that both expresses and relies on a culture of openness, transparency, and humility. What comes after practice, and how decisions about hiring, evaluation, and implementation make the work you do more effective, is the focus of the sixth chapter, and in the final chapter we reflect more extensively on the application and importance of practice in achieving better results in professional endeavors.

RETHINKING
PRACTICE

Malcolm Gladwell's widely read book *Outliers* is, you could argue, a study of the number 10,000. That's the amount of practice, in hours, necessary to become world-class at just about anything, he argues. Gladwell details how the "10,000 hour rule" helps to explain the rise of experts from Bill Gates to the Beatles. Exceptional talent equals an exceptional quantity of practice—10,000 hours to be exact. But of course what you do in practice matters as much as, if not more than, how much you practice. "A kid who practices hours of sloppy pick-up basketball every day is going to develop less than a kid who practices really well for two hours a day with good instruction and feedback," Michael Goldstein, one of the best teacher trainers in the country, recently told us. John Wooden seems to concur, offering would-be coaches this singular advice: "Never mistake activity for achievement."

On the basketball court, in the classroom, and in a thousand other places, you can work hard without getting very far. During practices, coaches urge hustle and effort, but they aren't enough, a fact that is especially challenging because hard work is so easy to see. Like a shiny, bright, and brilliantly distracting object, it draws our attention. We overrate hard work in evaluating the effectiveness of practice. "Bustling bodies making noise can be deceptive,"

Wooden wrote. Hustle and bustle can distract us from noticing when we're not actually that productive. This is just one of the ways that this chapter asks you to reexamine assumptions and truisms about how practice works.

Let's begin by looking at a youth sports practice. It is a brisk evening and a group of nine-year-old soccer players are bustling about on a patch of turf. The drill they're doing requires them to dribble the ball through a set of cones, then pass the ball underneath a bench as they run to one side of it, meeting the ball on the other side. Once they do this they move into a square of cones where they tap the ball back and forth between both feet quickly ten times. Next they race off to a new set of cones where they tap the top of the ball with alternating feet. The sequence ends with their dribbling in for a shot on goal. At first glance, the drill seems first-rate. It offers constant activity and continuous variation plus the opportunity to practice a myriad of skills. Busy bees! A closer look, however, reveals that what these players are doing may not lead to much improvement. It's not enough to just be busy.

Consider the part of the drill in which players tap the ball back and forth between both feet, for example. One of the keys to doing the activity correctly is to bend the knees slightly, as one of the coaches points out when she introduces the drill. However, you observe that many of the players complete the activity with their knees locked. Some appear to pass the ball fairly well, but in reality they are practicing doing it wrong, getting better at standing up straight instead of flexing their knees. Every time they run through the drill, they get more and more familiar with the feel of playing with their knees locked. As they do so, they get further and further from their goal. Now think of all the skills contained within these drills and all the ways players might be doing them wrong—shooting with a loose ankle or pushing the ball too far ahead on the dribble, and so on. Activity? Yes. Achievement? Not so much.

Surely the practice we just described isn't all that bad, but it could be much better. Training and development of an organization's talent that is "merely good" is not enough to make individuals or an organization significantly better than anyone else. Even a higher quantity of "good" practice won't really set your organization apart. To be significantly better you need to be significantly more productive in every minute that you practice. You need to be great. Fortunately, great is often not that far from good, and even small changes can increase by a striking degree the rate at which people develop.

Michael Goldstein applies this idea to teacher training. He observed to educator-writer Jay Mathews recently that less practice of better quality could yield more preferable results than more practice of lesser quality: "A rookie teacher who simply student teaches or acts as an assistant teacher might simply be repeating the WRONG moves." Imagine the benefits to the teaching field, Goldstein wonders, if the same amount of practical learning could be accomplished in a practice lab at one fifth the cost of a typical field placement, or at the same cost with five times the learning. And imagine the squandered investment. We send teachers out to "practice" the job in settings where there's not much supervision or specificity about what and how; not much feedback and oversight. We know the cost of training is immense, but for all we know, it doesn't help at all. Couldn't a similar argument be made about the training of doctors and lawyers and a thousand other professionals?

In the rules that follow we'll rethink eight assumptions many people hold about practice (and see the summary table at the end of the chapter). Reexamining assumptions can help you dramatically improve the quality of what you do to get your team ready for the game, a key meeting, a challenging work situation, an artistic performance, or a medical procedure. In all of those cases better practice will help you to win.

In reading this chapter, your goal need not be to turn what you do for practice upside down all at once so much as to tinker and improve it, piece by piece, to find what works better, until what you have is a killer app for improving people. See if this works. If so, keep it. You can be skeptical and still test new ideas, then decide whether each one is the right change to drive results. So choose an idea, maybe even a handful, and see where that takes you. These rules will start you on your journey.

RULE 1
ENCODE SUCCESS

We are fond of saying "practice makes perfect," and indeed the title of this book plays on the connection between practice and perfection. But it is more accurate to say that practice makes permanent. In practice you can master a skill thoroughly or not at all, and what you master can be the correct method or one where your knees are locked. Either way, what you do is likely to become encoded—it will be instilled in muscle memory or mental circuitry and become habit—for better or worse. Practice all the wrong moves and your team will execute the wrong moves when it's time to perform. Practice without intentionality and you will perform without much intentionality. A critical goal of practice, then, should be ensuring that participants encode success—that they practice getting it right—whatever "it" might be. While that may sound obvious, practice that encodes failure is common. There are a lot of reasons for this, but two seem especially pervasive. First, we can fail to observe our practices carefully and strategically enough to see whether participants are getting things right, and second, we can put participants in situations that make failure likely in a mistaken effort to steepen the learning curve. In a minute we'll tell you a bit more about those two pitfalls but first, a brief digression on the topic of romanticizing failure.

Someone you know, maybe your Uncle Lou, tells a version of this story. He will be thinking back to the days when he was just learning to (a) write a legal brief, (b) ride a bike, (c) dance the tarantella, or (d) shingle a roof, and say, "By God, I tried it a hundred times. Got it wrong the first ninety-nine, but I picked myself up. Eventually I got it." Your Uncle Lou may be right that he learned that skill pretty well, and the struggle may have been invaluable to him—but just because a great many things have been learned via Uncle Lou's method does not mean that it is the most efficient and effective way to learn in general. Uncle Lou may have learned at a cost, in time and effort, that was ten times what was necessary. Which means that the real story could equally have been how good he might have been if he'd learned more efficiently. If your job or your passion is to make success systematic, to train people to do something better than anyone else—value investment cash flows, teach public school children, field ground balls cleanly—be skeptical of stories that romanticize failure. While failure may build character and tenacity, it's not as good at building skills.

Let's look more closely at those two common reasons why practice encodes failure. The first comes about because running effective practice requires a systematic attentiveness to participants' rate of success. "You haven't taught it until they've learned it," Wooden liked to say, and the best teachers test to see how much students have learned—a process called "checking for understanding"—every few seconds. They realize that lack of understanding builds on itself and gets harder to fix the longer you wait, so they are always asking themselves, "Are students getting it? Am I sure?" In the case of practice, systematic observation of participants to ensure that they can do what you tried to teach them should include not just checking but acting on the results. Practice should be designed so that a participant who fails to succeed at an activity tries it over again. This can be within the activity's original setting (they go back to the front of the line) or in an impromptu one-on-one session ("Let's try that a few times standing right over here, Charles"). Checking for mastery requires responding to failure to remediate it as quickly and as positively as you can. But it also means thinking differently. It means thinking about participant performance as data. If you were running a practice session and three participants got the activity wrong followed by one who got it right, you might be tempted to think, "Good, they finally got it." It's just as plausible that the correct response would be, "Uh-oh. Only one out of four of them got it." In other words, the news is cause for concern, not celebration. In the soccer practice we described at the beginning of the chapter, players encoded dribbling a soccer ball wrong and therefore got better at doing it wrong. One contributing factor was the drill's design, which made it difficult for coaches and players to be attentive to whether success was happening—to check for mastery. With five different activities going on at once there was probably too much for the coaches to process with the kind of systematic, data-driven focus that checking for mastery requires. Every time they turned, there was a new thing to be looking for: locked ankles, bent knees, being up on toes. The result was lack of awareness about participants' level of mastery of each task. The complexity of the drill increased the likelihood that failure went undiagnosed—and thus continued.

Another source of encoded failure is the tendency of coaches to double down on difficulty in the hope that this will steepen the learning curve. If hitting a hundred pitches in the backyard will make your daughter a better hitter, it's easy to think that hitting a hundred 60-mile-per-hour pitches in a batting cage will make her better even faster, but that's not true. Facing pitches that are moderately above her current ability level is likely to allow your daughter to apply small corrections to what she does and see whether they work. It allows her to get more efficient with her technique. However, if the pitches are too fast and result in her consistently missing the ball, she's likely to start reaching desperately to make contact, disrupting the things she already does well and trying random rather than productive adaptations. Straining fruitlessly at the streaking ball, she risks developing new bad habits.

Cognitive scientist Daniel Willingham observes in his book *Why Don't Students Like School?* that people learn fastest when the problem solving they are asked to do requires them to make small and steady leaps, when problems are challenging but not sink-or-swim-ish. If the task is accelerated too much, learning slows down. What's more, Willingham observes, people like solving problems when they are presented in a gradual and incrementally more complex way, which means people are actually happy when they are learning well. But this means that failure can also be costly. It may cause participants to give up. Only by immense forces of will do they keep going when they get it wrong time and again. The fact that Uncle Lou remembers his desperate, knocked-down-99-times struggle to learn so vividly only suggests that it was perhaps the only time in his life when he endured such a struggle.

Finally, it is important to consider what we mean by success. While we want participants to experience primarily success during practice, the ideal success rate still isn't 100 percent—if that's the case, then the activity isn't hard enough. You want a success rate that's high enough to be reliable: most of the participants get it right most of the time. If you start a process with a significant amount of error, don't stop until your participants have begun to encode success. If the error is persistent and prevalent, ask yourself whether there needs to be so much of it. Why not redesign the process instead, eliminating complexity or variables to make the task temporarily simpler, breaking a chain of skills down to focus on just one, or slowing things down so there's time to process the complexity and then speeding it up later on? As a rule of thumb, we use the following goal for practice: you want your participants to complete the fastest possible right version of the activity. If they aren't able to do it right, slow down and work back up to the original task. A corollary of this is to do the most complex possible right version your participants are able to sustain with consistent—if imperfect—success. If they aren't able to do it right, eliminate complexity until you start to see mastery. Then build back up from there.

Encode Success

- Engineer practice activities so that the success rate is reliably high; if the activities are especially challenging, ensure that they end with a period of reliable success so your participants practice getting it right.

- Check for mastery constantly. If activities don't result in reliable success, simplify temporarily so that participants start successful; then add complexity.
- Focus participants on the "fastest possible correct version" or the "most complex right version possible" for any activity.

RULE 2
PRACTICE THE 20

The 80/20 rule, commonly cited among economists to explain a wide variety of events, is sometimes known as the "law of the vital few." It's a pattern that holds true again and again: 80 percent of results turn out to come from 20 percent of the sources. Your business digs into the data and finds that 80 percent of its profits come from 20 percent of its customers. Or in seeking to understand those high-value customers, the company finds that 80 percent of the useful information comes from 20 percent of the data points. Even though you spend a ton of money gathering the rest of the data, it doesn't actually help you that much.

The law of the vital few relates to practice as well. It suggests that to become great, you should focus more on practicing the 20 percent of things that most create value than the other 80 percent of things you could plausibly spend time on. You'd practice that 20 percent of things obsessively—80 percent of the time, some would argue—eschewing things of lesser value and becoming, metaphorically (or literally), the football team that runs five plays so well that even when everyone in the stadium knows they're coming, they're still unstoppable. With practice you'll get stronger results if you spend your time practicing the most important things.

One of the most counterintuitive but valuable things we've realized about practice is that the value of practicing something *increases* once you've mastered it. Most people say, when participants get to proficiency, "Good, they know how to do that. Now let's move on." But if you are practicing one of those most important skills—one of the 20 percent of skills that drive 80 percent of results—don't stop when your participants "know how to do it." Your goal with these 20 percent skills is excellence, not mere proficiency. Keep going so that what you develop is automaticity, fluidity, and even, as we'll discuss later, creativity. Being great at the most important things is more important than being good at more things that are merely useful. Xavi Hernandez, one of the top soccer midfielders in the world, makes this point in an interview in England's *Guardian*. Xavi describes a single practice activity that characterizes Spanish soccer and explains its dominance. "It's all about *rondos*," he says, referring to a game in which four or five players pass a ball rapidly around the outside of a square and one or two players pursue the ball. "*Rondo, rondo, rondo.* Every. Single. Day. It's the best exercise there is. You learn responsibility and not to lose the ball. If you lose the ball, you go in the middle. Pum-pum-pum-pum, always one touch." The drill is so useful that players do it over and over—at the expense of something new. The value of the drill doesn't decrease as they get better at it; it increases. And in the end the fact that the Spanish have a specific name for this drill expresses its importance—and, incidentally, the usefulness of naming drills to allow participants to discuss them more efficiently. To be, like the Spanish, the best in the world and to develop a competitive advantage, be alert for the times, when participants learn something in an especially valuable type of practice, when it would be more productive to say, "Good, let's keep practicing this until we're truly great."

So how do you find the 20 percent of the things that are the most important to practice? You may know these things already from experience. If so, great. If not, data can be an excellent source of insight. What do your customers tell you they appreciate? What do your employees say makes them value their managers? What math skills most lead to mastery of algebra a year from now?

What procedures in the operating room are most common—or are most likely to lead to errors, which could be eliminated?

If clear data are not available, consider harnessing the wisdom of crowds. We're stealing the phrase here from the book of the same name by *New Yorker* financial columnist James Surowiecki, who points out that aggregating the opinions of multiple people often yields an accurate analysis of a challenging situation—even if none of the people is an "expert." In one example, a missing submarine is found in the midst of thousands of square miles of open ocean by averaging the guesses of multiple scientists as to its location. No individual was close, but the average of all individual opinions was stunningly accurate.

If you're struggling to identify your 20 percent of things—if you don't know what the five most important things for a budding saxophonist to practice are—assemble a group of relatively informed people and ask them to name their top five. Using the five most frequently cited ideas as your answer won't be perfect, but it will be darned good and will allow you to begin practicing each topic to excellence. The goal is not to be good at basic skills and then move on. The goal, again, is to be great at the most important things.

It's worth noting that the 20 percent will change over time and thus require periodic reassessment. Assessing your 20 percent is also a smart way to use data. Tim Daly, president of The New Teacher Project, recently did this to revise the way his organization trains teachers. Daly realized that teachers TNTP placed in schools often never succeeded if they failed to learn to manage classroom behavior within the first two months. He asked his team to redesign training, dramatically reducing the number of topics on which new teachers received training and focusing on the skills they would need to establish a classroom culture until that goal was achieved. This change allowed them to spend 80 percent of their time on 20 percent of the skills and to better prepare their teachers for success. After that there would be more time, they realized, to practice skills that would be more important over the long run—a new 20 percent.

Your first instinct may be that organizing practices around the 80/20 rule will cause you to spend more time planning. The short answer is that you're probably right. You can't decide on Friday at 2 P.M. what you'll do for professional development that afternoon with your teachers; you can't decide each afternoon while driving to your daughter's basketball practice what you'll do at practice that day. The longer answer, however, is more nuanced. You have to build a map of your goals from the outset. And you have to design extremely high-quality activities for each of your 20-percenters that get progressively more complex. On the other hand, once you've done that, you'll no longer waste time preparing a smorgasbord of activities that you'll use briefly and discard. You invest in developing better activities that you will use over and over. In the end this may save you work.

Practice the 20
- Identify the 20 percent of things you could practice that will deliver 80 percent of the value.
- Practice the highest-priority things more than everything else combined.
- Keep practicing them: the value of practice begins at mastery!
- Save time by planning better in advance.
- Engage participants by repeating productive drills with minor variations instead of constantly introducing new ones.

RULE 3
LET THE MIND FOLLOW THE BODY

A colleague of ours, a teacher we'll call Sarah, spent a lot of time practicing giving directions to her students. She did this because students had sometimes struggled to follow her directions and several observers suggested that one reason might be the directions themselves: what Sarah asked her students to do was sometimes not so clear. So Sarah practiced, first writing out sequences of concrete, specific observable directions, a technique known as *What to Do* (described briefly at the end of this book). Then Sarah practiced saying aloud the directions she'd written as if she were delivering them to her class. She did this both on her own and with colleagues, and made revisions based on the surprising amount of insight she gained from hearing the words aloud. During the period of time when she was practicing her directions, she tried to make the skill a habit—that is, her natural way of thinking—so she practiced in every setting she could think of, even if only briefly.

A few weeks later, Sarah asked a colleague to observe her class. Afterwards, her colleague's first question was to ask Sarah herself how she thought it had gone. The good news, Sarah observed, was that the class had gone relatively well. Students had been orderly and productive, so at least she hadn't been embarrassed. But she apologized: she hadn't had a chance to try many *What to Dos* except at the beginning of class. She didn't demonstrate the skill she'd been practicing. Perhaps the observation had been a waste of time. Her observer had seen something totally different, however. She had seen Sarah use *What to Do* time and again when students needed a quick correction to help them back on task. Sarah, in short, had been using the thing she had practiced without even realizing it.

Sarah had made a habit of a skill through practice; in the game, when her mind was processing other things, it relied on the new habit without her realizing it. This experience may well be familiar to musicians and athletes and others who practice regularly. Once you have learned a skill to automaticity, your body executes, and only afterwards does your mind catch up. Customer service representatives who are trained to be calm with angry customers don't get any less frustrated in an adversarial situation; rather, they have normalized an emotionally constant response by practicing it. They do it without thinking, and this is exactly the point: the best way to get employees to behave calmly in the face of difficulty is not to ask them to consciously choose to exude calm during tense calls; it is, rather, to practice being calm in tense situations over and over so that it happens automatically.

In *Incognito: The Secret Lives of the Brain,* science writer David Eagleman describes not only the ways our brains do things we are not fully aware of, but the critical importance of our brains relying, entirely unconsciously, upon behaviors we've learned by rote. In one example, he describes research conducted on amnesia patients, whom researchers had learn and practice a video game. Because they had no short-term memory, they were unable to recall playing the game, but when they played again their scores improved at the same rate as those with fully functioning memories. The takeaway: You don't have to be aware of your knowledge to use it.

In fact, awareness often gets in the way. It is not a quirk of survival but a necessity that, speeding down the highway, your foot moves to the brake pedal well before your conscious brain has time to get involved in analyzing the decision. For people who perform for a living, the imperative of training the mind to execute unconsciously is also strong. Eagleman describes the ironic fact that "a professional athlete's goal is to not think." Rather, his goal is to develop "economical rote algorithms" during practice so that "in the heat of battle the right maneuvers will come automatically." Consider hitting a baseball. It takes about 0.4 seconds for a serious fastball to reach the plate. "Conscious awareness takes longer than that: about half a second," writes Eagleman, so most batters are not consciously aware of the ball's flight. The entire process happens before the batter becomes aware of it. Success is based on habits the batter has built but cannot consciously manage in the moment when they are most needed.

A synergy of conscious problem solving and automaticity developed through practice. This phenomenon is evident every time you drive. Not only do unconscious habits you've burned into your memory determine many of your actions, but while all of this is happening you may engage in some of your deepest and most reflective abstract thinking. While you are executing a series of complex skills and tasks that were at one time all but incomprehensible to you, your mind is free to roam and analyze and wonder. If you use practice to build mastery of a series of skills, and if you build up skills intentionally, you can master surprisingly complex tasks and in so doing free your active cognition to engage with other important tasks.

Our colleagues Nikki Frame and Maggie Johnson, you may recall, met for ten minutes every morning to practice responding to unexpected student answers. In the course of a few weeks, they managed to master the skill. One of the results was that Nikki and Maggie were left with additional processing capacity during class, which allowed them to focus on intellectually abstract and strenuous tasks.

Imagine how powerful this idea could be if applied in other highly technical or complex settings. Imagine doctors practicing, for a few minutes a few times a week, reacting calmly to agitated patients during examinations. Once they were able to do this with equanimity, it would both limit patient agitation and increase the processing capacity doctors had to listen to and assess their patients. They would solve complex problems at a higher rate by limiting the brain's focus on manageable aspects of the interaction. We will pick up this realization—that rote learning works in synergy with deep thinking—in our next rule, Unlock Creativity . . . with Repetition.

Let the Mind Follow the Body
- Stress learning skills all the way to automaticity so that participants can use them automatically—and before they consciously decide to.
- Build up layers of related automated skills so that participants can do complex tasks without actively thinking about them.

- Automate fundamentals, but also look for more complex and subtle skills that may also respond to automation. It's a false assumption that only simple things can become habits.

RULE 4
UNLOCK CREATIVITY . . . WITH REPETITION

Here's a useful observation from John Wooden that establishes a corollary to Rule 3: "Drilling creates a foundation on which individual initiative and imagination can flourish." If Rule 3 suggested the power of learning things by rote because it allows you to do them with unconscious efficiency, its corollary, Rule 4, focuses on what your conscious mind is doing while your unconscious mind is executing. To examine this, you might ask yourself when in the day you have your most creative thoughts. The answer is likely to be when you are taking a shower, driving your car, brushing your teeth, or jogging; that is, when you are doing some task you have done a thousand times and can complete automatically. What your mind is often doing when you are executing such tasks is thinking creatively. One way to get more creative is to give your mind the capacity to wander a little bit in settings where it had previously been encumbered—that is, by automating skills required in those settings.

Athletes and other performers often describe how, after a certain amount of experience and practice, the game "slows down" for them. What this means is that at certain points in the game their mind has gotten access to new processing capacity because complex actions have come to require a smaller percentage of available capacity. All of a sudden they can look up and see an open teammate or a new passing lane. This gives us more perspective on the connection between automaticity of high-frequency skills and creativity, a connection that Johann Cruyff makes even clearer.

Cruyff, counted among the five or so greatest soccer players of all time, is often cited for his unparalleled creativity. In a game, he would suddenly flout deeply rooted expectations about what to do in a certain situation and do something entirely unexpected—with devastating effect. In an interview, he was asked to recall players who, in his youth, were better than he was but who failed to succeed. Recalling them, he said, "They were very good players. But at a certain moment it has to be done quicker, where instead of having two meters to control the ball, you have half a meter and if the ball moves half a meter, you've lost it. When there was pressure it was all over. It had to be faster." Cruyff didn't say he had become more creative. Instead, he noted his automaticity at core skills—the 20 percent—under pressure. He was automatic and therefore prone to thinking about other things while executing. Creativity, it turns out, is often practice in disguise, and to get more of it, it often helps to automate other things. If you want to unlock creativity at certain critical moments, you might identify skills required at those moments and automate them in order to free up more processing capacity for creative thinking.

It's worth pausing here to observe that arguing in favor of more drilling would set many American educators on edge. Many educators perceive drilling—which they characterize with the pejorative "drill and kill"—to be the opposite, the enemy, of higher-order thinking. To them, an explicit correlation between imagination and drilling would be anathema. Learning that asks students to memorize and automate will reduce their ability to generate creative thoughts and make cognitive leaps, such educators might argue.

The problem with that argument is that learning generally doesn't work that way. As cognitive scientists like Daniel Willingham have shown, it's all but impossible to have higher-order thinking without strongly established skills and lots of knowledge of facts. Cognitive leaps, intuition, inspiration—the stuff of vision—are facilitated by expending the smallest possible amount of processing capacity on lower-order aspects of a problem and reapplying it at higher levels. You leap over the more basic work by being able to do it without thinking much about it, not by ignoring it. This synergy between the rote and the creative is more commonly accepted in many nations in Asia. "Americans have developed a fine dichotomy between rote and critical thinking; one is good, the other is bad," write the authors of one study[1] of Japanese schools. But they find that many types of higher-order thinking are in fact founded on and require rote learning. Creativity often comes about because the mind has been set free in new and heretofore encumbered situations.

In business school Doug once worked in a group trying to solve a macroeconomic problem. It came down to an equation made up of dozens of variables scrawled across a whiteboard. Solving it seemed impossible. Then, a member of the team—educated in Eastern Europe, not coincidentally—walked to the whiteboard. "This part of the equation must be negative," he said, circling a series of variables. "This coefficient is negative, and every other value is positive." He then circled two more strings of variables. "These two must be positive, because in this one all of the values are positive and in this one we multiply two negative values. So we have, really, in this equation a negative times two positives. This must give a negative." He sat down: "Like this, we will all go bankrupt." He had leapt over and across the problem in a way no one else had, not because he ignored the rote work but because he was so facile at it. To skip over the mundane parts you have to know them cold. John Wooden said that "[I] wanted to be as surprised as our opponent at what my team came up with when confronted with an unexpected challenge." What's counterintuitive is Wooden's belief about how you got there. Drilling let players' creativity emerge under pressure.

We began experimenting with the idea that increasing repetition could unlock creativity and individuality in our own teaching workshops and applied this idea to an activity called the "Strong

Voice" layup drill. In the activity (described in the back of the book), teachers practice prompting a slouching student to sit up. They cycle through a line playing the roles of teacher, student, and coach (who gives feedback). They practice using nonverbal skills to ensure compliance. The first time we ran the activity, we asked people to go through the line two or three times. What we saw was people doing something and thinking about it at the same time. Participants were completing the task but awkwardly and without adaptation to their own style and manner, so we made some simple changes.

First, we split groups in half. Instead of practicing in groups of eight, they practiced in groups of four. This doubled the repetitions each participant got. On the first try, participants were all over the map in their approaches; people tried using gestures that worked as often as they tried ones that didn't. They made sweeping, almost theatrical hand gestures, for example, that seemed strange and awkward. Over time, successful ideas began to emerge, and as a group they began to "get it," to internalize a vision of what the activity, well implemented, should look like: symmetrical posture and slow, controlled gestures. Variation decreased. People borrowed ideas from one another and began to look like each other. Some educators might have argued that the drill was causing creativity to decline. But then as we continued to practice, variation began to reemerge. Teachers made subtle changes to their gestures or their tone. Slowly, individuals developed their own style. Some were stricter; some were warmer. Some communicated with hand gestures; others gravitated to facial expression. Variation reemerged. Creativity was back—within a narrower range but with greater effectiveness.

After one workshop in which participants had completed perhaps fifteen iterations of the drill, one teacher made an especially insightful comment. On a final round of the activity, we asked teachers to assume that the student they were correcting was their most motivated and positive student, on a difficult day. "I felt like I was teaching from light," she said. "I was correcting, but it was positive—because I cared about her. I could feel the difference and I started to think, *My gosh, why don't I always teach from the light?"*

The three of us have returned to her observation time and again. We find it inspiring and powerful—in part because it is indicative of the type of people who teach and why we love the work so much, but also in part because it emerged from the meditative nature of practicing a mundane and unheralded moment, over and over. This insight might never have happened without an activity that may have at first appeared banal. Repetition gave rise to meditation and then wisdom.

Unlock Creativity . . . with Repetition

- Automate skills to free participants' cognition to be more creative.
- Look to automate skills at exactly the moments you need creativity most, to free up processing capacity.
- Push participants to reflect later, after they've practiced enough to better understand what they are doing.

RULE 5
REPLACE YOUR PURPOSE
(WITH AN OBJECTIVE)

Everyone has a purpose in mind when they lead practice, but to truly turn activity into achievement, replace your purpose with a clear and focused objective. The difference may seem semantic, but an objective is different from a purpose in four key ways.

The first difference between a purpose and an objective is that an objective is measurable. Having a purpose means knowing what you want to work on—passing, for example. Having an objective means defining specifically what your participants will be able to do by the end of the session—"be able to pass the ball accurately on the ground for distances of twenty yards." When an objective is measurable it means that at the end of the session you can tell, via observation or a quick assessment, whether you have succeeded at teaching it. You can't see whether your players can pass by the end of an hour: in what setting and under what circumstances do you mean? As a result you can't really tell whether you've accomplished anything. By contrast, you *can* see whether players can consistently pass the ball accurately over distances of twenty yards on the ground, though measuring that might cause you to get even more specific: "be able to pass the ball accurately on the ground for distances of twenty yards so the receiving player does not have to adjust his position on eight out of ten tries." Framing your goal precisely and measurably lets you understand more clearly what your players can do and how effective your teaching was, and allows you to set high standards—"we're not done until we get it eight of ten times."

Second, an objective should be manageable: you should be able to accomplish it in the time available. You couldn't expect players to master the skill of passing in an hour of practice; they'll spend years mastering all of its nuances and skills and settings. But depending on the skills they've mastered in previous sessions, you might hope to have them master a singular aspect of passing. And only by knocking down all the pieces of passing effectively, day by day, will they master the larger art.

Here's what those first two criteria might look like in a professional setting. If you were working with a group of surgical residents, you would replace a purpose like "We're going to practice preparing for surgery" with an objective: "We're going to practice applying our preoperative checklist with a full team, identifying and fixing small errors." That would be a focused objective. We'd bet on a team that addressed ten such precise objectives in sequence over a team that engaged in generalized practice ten times in a row.

In addition to being manageable and measurable, an objective should also come with mastery guidance—one or two things to focus on in doing it right. You tell your surgical residents, "to do it right you want to focus on getting your light source shining down on the incision, and to use standardized signals to ask team members to adjust lighting." In the case of passing the ball accurately on the ground over long distances, you'd want your players to focus on locking their ankle when striking the ball and following through with their knee raised. This allows participants to practice with focus and intentionality and to concentrate on successful execution versus mere completion of an activity.

Last, an effective objective is made ahead of practice, and this is perhaps the biggest challenge of all. Many practices begin with the thought, "What am I going to do tomorrow?" (or even this afternoon!). When you ask this question, you are starting with an activity, not an objective—with the action, not the reason for it. In the end, you can't decide if an activity is the right one to do until you know why you're doing it. Instead, start by asking what you are going to accomplish, and then ask what the best route to that goal is. When an objective is made first, before the activity, it guides you in choosing or adapting your activities. When it comes second, after you decide what you'll do, it is a justification.

This may seem like an esoteric difference, but it isn't. We once videotaped a champion teacher in his classroom, a guy who amidst a school of "pretty good" had achieved consistently outstanding results among his students. After taping his class, we lingered to watch a training session run by the principal of the school, who asked the staff to write down the percentage of their planning time they used to plan their lesson and the percentage to define their objective. The principal went around the room asking teachers to share what they wrote. "Ninety percent of my time on the lesson activities, ten percent on the objective," said one teacher. Another said 95 and 5; a third, 80 and 20. The principal came to the teacher we'd taped, the champion teacher: "Ten or twenty percent of my time on the activities," he said, "eighty or ninety percent of my time on the objective." Great teachers understand that you start with the outcome you desire. The strategic decision about what skill to refine is the essence of teaching. When we would practice responding to off-task student behavior via a drill we called "behavior lab," one teacher, like Jen in the story from the Introduction, would stand at the front of the room and try to teach while the rest of us played students—some being productive, some disruptive. But we were not at first specific enough about what we were working on, and so teachers would face a random set of behaviors to address—not what they had reflected on, not what they were especially weak or strong at. Lacking intentionality, we failed to make teachers much better. Over time we learned to set particular objectives: sometimes for each session of behavior lab, sometimes for each round, occasionally for each participant. Our results improved immensely.

A final observation is necessary here. A good objective operates in concert with other objectives. It builds on skills your participants have recently mastered and leads to more comprehensive and complex areas of mastery. Your objectives may involve learning nothing new except integrating skills your participants mastered previously. As you strive to reach this point of integration, perhaps some aspect will appear especially difficult and will require further attention—that is, another practice session that repeats the original objective. Your purpose adapts then to the rate of mastery demonstrated in practice, and you aren't afraid to circle back and repeat a topic, possibly multiple times.

Replace Your Purpose (with an Objective)

- Replace the vague idea of a "purpose" with a manageable and measurable objective that is made ahead of practice and gives mastery guidance.
- Teach skills in a sequence of objectives of increasing complexity.

- Include objectives that focus on integrating previously mastered skills.
- Adapt objectives to the rate of participants' mastery.

LEARNINGS: UNDER SIX SECONDS

Caleb Porter, coach of the United States Under-23 National Soccer Team, sets a measurable goal for his players, not only in practice but in games. Any time they lose possession of the ball, they must do anything they can to win it back within six seconds. If they fail, they return after that to "normal" defensive strategy. While most coaches tell their teams to work hard to win the ball back after they lose it, Porter's goal, adapted from one used by top coaches in Spain, is measurable and the difference is important. With a more general goal of working hard to win the ball back, players would likely believe they had accomplished the goal in every situation. Doesn't every player believe he or she worked hard to get the ball back? Porter's objective, by contrast, allows him to hold his players more accountable—because it is objective. It also allows him to set measurable goals. He could set a goal of earning the ball back in the first six seconds 60 percent of the time—during a game or during practice. He could support it with what teacher trainer Michael Goldstein calls "feedback with a number." "We achieved our six-second goal 40 percent of the time." This allows players to constantly know where they stand and for the coach to set goals without always being the source of the judgment. It's very different to say, "We won the ball back 40 percent of the time. We need to win it back 60 percent of the time. Let's keep working," than it is to say, "We didn't work hard enough to win the ball back. We need to practice working harder." The team can run drills with exactly the same objective it'll have during their games.

RULE 6
PRACTICE "BRIGHT SPOTS"

One purpose for practice is to help people get better at things they can't yet do. This type of practice plays an important role in our lives: we look for areas that need improvement and work on them. But it's important not to get stuck in a deficit mindset. Using practice to get even better at the things we're already good at is also a powerful opportunity.

In *Switch*, Dan and Chip Heath coined the phrase "Bright Spots" to talk about the often overlooked and underleveraged power of what works. It's easy, they note, to bewail what's wrong rather than see the power of what's right. We borrow their term to remind ourselves that in a practice setting, immense value can be realized by focusing on things participants are already good at—and making them even better.

One of the most reassuring aspects of Doug's study of high-performing teachers was the realization that champions—teachers who were positive anomalies in the field—were just like the rest of us in many ways. They too had weaknesses. Sometimes they explained things poorly. Their lesson plans had gaps some days too. What differentiated outstanding teachers most was how dynamic their strengths were. Consider one math teacher, who we'll call Bill and who achieved breathtaking results year after year. His math knowledge had occasional gaps in it, and he was decently organized but not outstandingly so. Sometimes he realized, standing in front of class, that he had forgotten to copy something he needed. Sometimes a problem he put in his lesson plan didn't pan out. What made Bill outstanding was his gift for inspiring students to give their best. Combined with energetic pacing, this engaged students in class and ensured that they happily completed problem after problem. You could sense the power of Bill's strengths as soon as you entered his room: there was a buzz, an urgency, that exuded from the smallest actions of the most challenged students, and the power of these things trounced the times when Bill had to ask a student to go make a copy for him. In fact, there were many teachers like Bill; only their profile of strengths and weaknesses differed. One might be a bit weak in the area of motivating and inspiring students, perhaps, but was a world-class lesson planner.

One conclusion you could draw from this is that if you wanted to make more game-changing teachers, you might obsess a little less on mitigating every weakness and focus more on maximizing strengths, on getting them so good that they override weaknesses. If a participant notes that he or she is already good at something you propose to practice, it's usually in an effort to avoid practicing it, but in fact it's all the more reason to practice—because practicing strengths is more likely to make them great. As an added bonus practicing strengths helps us remember what we are good at and feel positively about the profession or performance at which we hope to excel. The more people enjoy practicing, the more they will do it, and the better they'll get. Having strong presenters practice presenting can make them feel even more confident and joyful. You might give them advanced presentation formats in which to apply their skills, or assign other job tasks where their presentation skills might be applicable. Spotting things that people are good at and finding ways to use those skills more broadly is one of the most productive things an organization can do for an employee, or that practice can do for a participant.

Practicing bright spots can be particularly effective when practicing as a team. In any one team, chances are that not everyone shares the same strengths; one person's bright spot becomes another person's model, which can be very valuable to the entire team (for more on modeling see the third chapter). The whole team benefits. The person who demonstrated gets the opportunity to shine and to feel the respect of peers. He also gets even better, as performing in front of peers who are insiders and know the difference between good and great can raise the level of performance as well as the quality of feedback. The team is strengthened by these reminders that their colleagues bring important skills to the work they share. Everyone is inspired to strive for excellence.

Practice "Bright Spots"
- Identify and practice areas of talent as well as areas of weakness.
- Seek ways to apply established skills in new settings to leverage strengths.
- Use one participant's strengths to model for other team members and speed replication across the group.

LEARNINGS: YOUR BEST STUFF (AND NAMING IT)

Legions of coaches seek to make practice interesting by "changing things up" constantly and introducing new drills. There are times and places where this makes sense; too much repetition can be boring. But good practice activities appreciate in value the more you use them. Rather than wearing out, they get better. Repeating high-quality activities has lots of advantages, including in many cases increased enjoyment for participants.

The more you repeat an activity, the better your participants get at doing it. You avoid tedious time spent learning simply how to complete the activity. Using a familiar activity, or a minor adaptation of one, you can skip the long descriptions and demonstrations required to roll out something new. Participants can do the activity right the first time without false starts and errors. They are familiar with the logistics of the activity (like where to stand and what will happen next) and therefore can focus on the skill they are learning. If you're worried that this may make your practices less interesting, you might be wrong. Being a part of a practice where you are active, busy, and know what to do is just as likely to be more engaging than a practice beset by a lack of productivity.

It's also worth doing what John Wooden did: keeping track of your best activities and reflecting on what worked. As you make minor tweaks to improve them, the value will go up. The fourth time you do an activity is far more valuable than the first. By then you will have refined

(Continued)

it to be most effective and efficient, with minor kinks worked out. See your best activities as assets and invest in them over time.

The last step may be giving your practice activities names. This allows you to talk about them efficiently ("We're going to use feedback here in much the same way we do in our Strong Voice layup drill"), and it allows people to begin doing them at a minimum transaction cost: "Ten minutes of the Layup Drill . . . Go!"

RULE 7
DIFFERENTIATE DRILL FROM SCRIMMAGE

George has recently been promoted to principal at his school and is about to facilitate his first staff meeting. There is a lot riding on it. He will be setting precedents for his leadership and the way he hopes the faculty will work together. The challenge is to facilitate the meeting efficiently and drive a high-quality discussion that addresses real organizational challenges, all while making sure that his team comes to believe that he listens carefully and values their ideas. In preparation for the meeting, he completes two activities, allowing him to practice in important, but different ways. First, working on his own, he goes through the meeting agenda and, for each segment where he will ask for input or comments, writes out possible responses from faculty members, each response on a note card. He then flips through them, reading them one at a time out loud and practicing responding with active listening skills—restating the comment or highlighting some part of it to show that he took it seriously, even if he disagreed. When his tone feels off or his comments poor, he immediately doubles back and answers the card a second time. He goes through the stack of cards several times, drilling himself until active listening feels natural.

Next, George enlists Carly, the principal of a nearby school, to help. She asks him to run through the whole meeting from top to bottom, pretending that it's the real thing. She plays the part of different meeting participants, chiming in during the participatory moments with a variety of comments—some from George's note cards and others of her own. She varies the tenor and tone: sometimes enthusiastic, sometimes skeptical, sometimes feigning confusion. In this practice, however, she discourages George from stopping midstream to revise a response. George has to practice implementing all of the skills he's been working on in real, sustained time, with all of the unpredictability of participants' moods and all of the distractions of following the agenda and running the meeting. It's a sort of rehearsal.

The two forms of practice illustrate the difference between drill and scrimmage. The first activity was a drill. A drill deliberately distorts the setting in which participants will ultimately perform in order to focus on a specific skill under maximum concentration and to refine that skill intentionally. Drills strive to maximize the amount of mental energy focused on a skill. They increase density, the number of productive iterations of a skill per minute of practice. In the actual meeting, George will not field comments in rapid succession; they'll be spread out. And he will not need to respond to every comment, nor will he use active listening every time. He certainly won't have opportunities to refine his responses. But in George's drill, he distorted the ultimate performance (the staff meeting) to concentrate on the area he needed to work on most. He amplified the number of comments he responded to and packed them together so that he could develop what David Eagleman calls "rote algorithms" through frequent, intentional, close-quarters repetition. He was able to immediately "fix" any answer he didn't like, so he encoded success. In short, he chose to develop skills by applying them in an artificial environment with intense focus. Had he merely performed the second activity, he would have had only a fraction of the opportunity to practice—not enough to develop proficiency.

A scrimmage, by contrast, is designed not to distort the game but to replicate its complexity and uncertainty. The practice that Carly helped George complete was designed to do this. Opportunities to work on active listening came about unpredictably, which gave George less practice but a better sense for whether his skills were meeting-ready—whether he could execute when he was distracted or didn't have advance warning. To this end Carly tried to replicate the involvement of multiple participants with different voices, styles, and agendas, just as George might find in the real meeting. During this scrimmage, Carly didn't let George stop and go back if he didn't like one of his answers. A scrimmage usually replicates key aspects of the performance's flow, like the sequence of key events, the amount of time you'll have, the location you'll perform in, or the distractions you might face. In some cases a scrimmage can heighten aspects of game conditions. Carly might have played the role of an especially difficult faculty member, for example, one tougher to handle than most if not all George was likely to face. Or, during a scrimmage, a pro sports team might broadcast excessive crowd noise to prepare its players for distraction. The distinction between drill and scrimmage is imperfect, but remains important. Among other things, the purposes are different, for drills focus on skill development and scrimmages on evaluation and final preparation. You use the former to focus maximum attention on the thing you want to learn, and the latter to answer questions: Are you ready to play the game or run the meeting? Which members of your team are prepared? Whose mindset responds best to the pressure of performance?

When and how much should we drill? When is scrimmage the best choice? Wooden again provides some insight. Given the benefits of twenty players on the court with five balls in an engineered and predictable learning environment as compared to ten players on the court with one ball in an unpredictable series of interactions, the "Wizard of Westwood" consciously chose to drill more—and scrimmage less—than most coaches. He was aware of the discrepancy and thought it was a key factor in his teams' success. Wooden reserved scrimmaging for evaluating his players. Once he knew where they stood, he preferred to focus on maximizing teaching and learning. This is important. While scrimmaging is often fun, its ease of use makes it easy to rely on and can lead to a practice without a clear objective.

Some coaches also believe that scrimmage is the only way to teach participants to integrate skills. Drills can easily integrate skills, however. Indeed, a whole category of drills integrates previously mastered skills. For example, before engaging in a full-on scrimmage with Carly, George might have added a second drill in which he tried to integrate active listening and redirection of off-topic comments. In such a drill, Carly might have mixed in comments that threatened to take George off topic with those which presented opportunities for active listening. This may seem like overkill, but consider the value. After initial drilling, many people are eager to take their skills into the game or engage in scrimmage, but often this doesn't go smoothly. It can be frustrating and chaotic. A graduated practice is what sets the champion coaches in all fields apart from the merely good.

Differentiate Drill from Scrimmage
- Use drills to distort the game and focus intensively on development of one or several skills.
- Use scrimmages to evaluate your readiness for performance.
- Recognize that scrimmaging is generally less efficient as a teaching tool.
- Recognize that success in scrimmage is the best indicator of true mastery—participants can perform a skill when the time and place of its application is unpredictable.
- Consider using a sequence of drills that integrate new skills with previously mastered skills before—or in lieu of—scrimmage.

RULE 8
CORRECT INSTEAD OF CRITIQUE

John Wooden said, about practice, that no error should go uncorrected. Armed with this insight, you might be inclined to set up practice so that every time a player made a mistake you pulled her aside and said, "Quicker and sharper cuts, Luisa!" Would that give you incredible results? Maybe. But what Wooden wanted was correction, not critique, and the difference is that critique involves telling a participant how to do it better but correction means going back and doing it again, and doing it better—as soon as possible. So in an ideal practice, a player might go right back into the line and practice cutting more sharply, say. Only when she has done correctly what was at first erroneous has correction been accomplished. Practice, as we've pointed out, is about inscribing habits on the brain through repetition with variation. What makes you execute an action in performance is having done it in practice. So critique—merely telling someone that she did it wrong— doesn't help very much. Only correction, doing it over again right, trains people to succeed.

It may be worth reflecting that the body's neural circuits have very little sense of time. If you do it right once and wrong once, it's encoded each way equally in your neural circuitry. It may matter little which one happened first. The ratio is one to one. If you are correcting, then, correct in multiples. If one of your tennis players hits backhand incorrectly, doing it right once will help erase the error, but doing it right three or four times right away will begin to overwhelm the wrong memory with the right one. Think about saying, after an error in corrected, "Yes. Good. Now do it five more times!"

Earlier, in our discussion of Rule 4, we told you about our own version of the classic basketball layup drill—a drill in which teachers practice using the technique Strong Voice to ask a student to sit up. They roll through the drill multiples times, often with different iterations, asking the slouching student to sit up by employing elements of body language and tone of voice.

As we ran this activity, we often noticed the time lag between our critique and the correction step. Participants heard our advice—"Keep your body symmetrical; try not to tilt your head"— and went to the back of the line. Sometimes we ran out of time before people got a chance to try again, however, and sometimes the participant's memory of the incident wasn't fresh by the time they got another chance. We began sending people to the front of the line instead. This let them try it right away and feel themselves getting better in the span of a minute. This is one way to turn critique into correction and make correction happen quickly and with greater accountability. It's worth noting that the process of correction does not even require a coach. Self-correction, the process of observing our own subpar demonstration of a skill and repeating the action more effectively, ideally multiple times, is forever open to us.

Correct Instead of Critique

- Strive to ask participants to redo an action differently or better rather than just telling them whether or how it could have been different.
- Try to shorten the feedback loop and achieve correction as quickly as possible after an action that requires intervention.
- Always maintain a teaching mentality and focus on the solution ("cut more sharply to the basket") rather than the problem ("your cut wasn't sharp").
- Seek opportunities to correct privately. When you correct publicly, make it clear that it's a common error, then make sure to correct, not critique, by asking all participants to repeat the action.

RETHINKING ASSUMPTIONS ABOUT PRACTICE

Rule	Assumption	Reexamination
Encode success	Practice makes perfect. Work hard and you'll improve.	Practice makes permanent. Practice can be unproductive or even counterproductive unless you practice doing it right.
Practice the 20	Practice as many useful skills as you can.	Practice fewer, more important things, better and more deeply.
Let the mind follow the body	Prepare to perform by preparing yourself to make decisions during the game.	Prepare to perform by preparing yourself not to have to make decisions during the game.
Unlock creativity . . . with repetition	Rote learning gets in the way of higher-order thinking.	Higher-order thinking relies on rote learning. Automaticity frees your mind to create.
Replace your purpose (with an objective)	You should have a purpose for your activities during practice.	You should have an objective that is manageable, measurable, made first, and includes mastery guidance.
Practice "bright spots"	Use practice to fix what you're not good at.	Use practice to get better at things you already do well.
Differentiate drill from scrimmage	Practice activities are best when they replicate as many aspects as possible of the performance itself—that is, when they are scrimmages.	Drills—which isolate a skill—are often more productive than scrimmages, specifically because they distort the game.
Correct instead of critique	Feedback automatically helps people get better.	Using feedback and doing it over again makes people better.

HOW TO PRACTICE

On May 2, 2011, members of the United States Special Forces landed under cover of night at a strange and heavily bunkered compound in Abbottabad, Pakistan. You know by now how things panned out. The nation's bravest and best-trained soldiers ably executed a dangerous and critical mission culminating in the death of Osama bin Laden and—at least as important it turns out—the capture of reams of information that have compromised al-Qaeda operations around the globe. The raid constitutes a bright spot for our military forces and our nation. In some ways we take the sort of flawless execution we imagine from the SEAL team members who landed that night for granted. They are our best and our brightest, our most indefatigable, and trained to execute this kind of operation. They underscore this perception; on the rare occasions when they speak about it, you're almost assured of hearing something like, "We've trained all our lives for this kind of thing. It's what we do."

It is easy to expect this kind of performance from our Special Forces. They are the elite of our military. Yet, consider the events of April 24, 1980, when a Special Forces team attempted to rescue 52 American hostages in Iran. A sandstorm and a broken hydraulic system began a downward spiral of catastrophe that ended with the collision of a helicopter and a transport plane, the deaths of eight American servicemen, a disastrous blow to

American prestige, and the continuation of the Iran Hostage Crisis. What made the difference between success and disaster by highly trained experts? Certainly not just the accidents of helicopter crashes and wind storms. After all, the mission in Abbottabad began with one of just two helicopters crashing into the compound itself.

After the failed mission in 1980, a White House commission set out to understand what had gone wrong and to reconsider how the command prepared the Special Forces team in order to prevent a similar disaster. The commission prompted rethinking by the Joint Special Forces Operations Command, which then made concrete changes in the way it prepared for these missions. In preparing for the mission in Pakistan, it gathered extensive intelligence on all aspects of the mission, including bin Laden's specific location, the detailed layout of the compound, and exactly whom else they would expect to be inside. In Rule 9, "Analyze the Game," we will pick up this idea that you must first know exactly what outstanding performance requires before you dive into practice. The SEAL team also practiced the operation, over and over again. They built a full-scale replica of the bin Laden compound at Bagram Air Force Base in Afghanistan. They practiced for weeks in the replica compound, preparing for details such as the direction in which a doorknob would open to ensure that they weren't distracted by mundane complications as they focused on key strategic goals during the actual operation. This is an idea we will examine more in Rule 12, "Integrate the Skills." In short, they operationalized the new principles, and as a result, the diligence and humility of the nation's best soldiers in preparing through effective practice resulted in one of the most successful days in recent memory for American forces.[1]

We too have learned from struggle. We recognize that while we made dramatic shifts in our *thinking* of what constitutes effective practice, the most important shifts we made were in *how* we practiced. Some of these shifts were seemingly subtle, such as giving our techniques and skills, as well as the drills we use to practice them, names. Some changes have been more intensive, such as redesigning our drills to first isolate and then integrate skills. Some of these changes have been easy, while others we resisted.

The key to moving from rethinking your practice to executing effective practice is that it is not enough to know how you want it to look. Your ideas have to translate to concrete action. Prepare to roll up your sleeves and design practice that yields results. Here's how.

RULE 9
ANALYZE THE GAME

Potentially the most important rule for how to practice is to know what it takes to be great. Whatever your field, a disciplined approach to identifying top performers and analyzing top performance provides you with the curriculum. The skills you see in your top performers are the very skills you then work to develop in everyone on your team. This knowledge doesn't just come with experience. Experience is important, but unless that experience is studied and analyzed carefully to uncover the factors that actually contribute to greatness, its potential is limited to a chance match between insight and application.

The story of the transformation of the Oakland A's entered our national consciousness through the best-selling book and major motion picture *Moneyball.* Eschewing the tendencies of scouts and coaches to overpersonalize their view of the game, A's manager Billy Beane and his assistant Paul DePodesta studied the game and analyzed stats. As journalist Michael Lewis describes in the book, the Oakland A's were able to identify talent that had been lying fallow, buy it cheap, and develop it to create a team that could compete with the Yankees at a fraction of the cost. The key was not trying to acquire stars but to understand better than anyone else who the real stars were by understanding the skills that actually won games. The old talent scouts, the ones with the deep experience, were looking for star power, for something intangible that they were convinced separated the great from the not-so-great. Meanwhile, A's manager Billy Beane, armed with data and looking for concrete skills that other teams had overlooked— getting on base, or taking lots of pitches rather than swinging— succeeded in building a winning team on the cheap.

Analyzing the game allows you not only to break down the specific skills that point the way to success but to understand the role they play, to prioritize and rank. Beane and DePodesta wanted players who took pitches rather than just swung. They knew that the players who demonstrated discipline at the plate and took more pitches (even if that meant they didn't get a hit) often had a higher rate of getting on base. And it seemed obvious yet overlooked that you had to get on base to score. One piece of data they collected on their players to understand their discipline at the plate was the rate of swinging at pitches that were outside the strike zone. They coached and coaxed and finally insisted that players stop swinging at bad pitches.

But given the amount of time they had spent trying to teach players plate discipline, and given that they hadn't learned it, Beane concluded that plate discipline was not something one could learn but was rather nearly a genetic trait.[2] He wrote off his ability to change his current players and placed more stock in his ability to recruit the type of players they were looking for.

But what if Beane were wrong? When *Moneyball* came out, it was read as a parable of selection and recruiting and seemed like a triumph of analysis over a game previously run on instinct. Yet, once Beane's recruiting analysis was made public, the success of the A's faded as other teams quickly replicated their recruitment strategy and began to beat them at the data game. What if Beane had analyzed further? What if he had developed the power of practice and his deep analysis had surfaced the specific behaviors and skills that went into plate discipline, skills that responded to practice? Interestingly, an interview later in the book reveals that perhaps it isn't that this skill of plate discipline can't be taught, but that it requires more analysis to understand exactly what builds plate discipline in those who have it.

The author interviews Scott Hatteberg, the player with the lowest percentage of swings at bad pitches. When Hatteberg describes his patience at the plate, he describes a different approach from simply waiting for the right pitch. He knew that the more he swung at balls, the greater the chance he would risk exposing his weakness, and once exposed he would either have to adjust his swing or lose his career. He therefore developed (1) his ability to hit almost anything, (2) his ability to know what pitches he could "do something with," or the pitches he should look for, (3) his ability to look for those pitches, and (4) his ability to spot and avoid those pitches he knew he couldn't do anything with.[3] It is possible that the insight Beane would have gained in analyzing players like Hatteberg—the list of more discrete, subtle, and potent skills that could be practiced in isolation—would have transformed the A's into a talent hotbed.

Our experience at Uncommon is not unlike that of Billy Beane in that we rely heavily on the research we've done to identify what goes into top performance. When our team first started observing the best teachers (teachers with the highest test results as well as the highest numbers of students living in poverty), we noted that these top performers were often unaware of the discrete skills they were using that yielded such great results, and indeed so were we. Regardless of their ability to self-reflect and improve, and regardless of their ability to reliably use a blend of powerful techniques, these teachers hadn't broken down the specific skills that went into their performance.

For Doug and the team he has brought together over the years to develop the techniques in *Teach Like a Champion*, it meant devoting several years to the work of watching and carefully parsing the work of the teachers who were getting the best results, and then parsing some more. It began with identifying a common ability in high performers—such as their ability to ask for and achieve 100%: 100% of students following their directions 100% of the way, 100% of the time. Next, Doug and the team observed that those teachers all used common principles to achieve that 100%. The team continued to analyze key moments and saw that there were specific types of corrections those teachers used, which were governed by one rule: always use the least invasive correction to achieve the desired result. When the team looked closely, they realized that there was a tremendous amount of finesse to this technique, and that it was made up of several discrete skills that could be taught.

Just imagine how powerful this information borne of detailed analysis of the game of teaching is. Without specific techniques to provide direction, we fall back on vague platitudes ("Teach from your heart!" "Mean business!" "Have high expectations!"— all equivalent to "Stop swinging at those pitches!") with the best intentions but a lack of actionable specifics. With slogans guiding the way, we make the assumption that the greatest lever to developing talent is motivation or mindset rather than specific actionable steps for incremental improvement. In our search to know what it takes to make teachers great, we first looked to the data to find the best teachers. Then we videotaped those teachers. Next we watched hundreds of hours of footage until commonalities and skills emerged. We described, discussed, and revised those observations. We put the techniques into action to see if they were truly the key skills and to understand what teachers needed to know in order to replicate the key techniques correctly. We showed top teachers the moments on video that we identified as moments of great technique, and they applied the models and improved them. It was a long, recursive process.

The result is a set of clearly defined techniques for becoming great at teaching (see Doug's book, *Teach Like a Champion*). This is the curriculum and starting point for us in developing our teachers—both those who have never taught before and those who have taught for years. It is our lens for continued practice and improvement, and our guide in developing our objectives for practice time with our staff. The first step for any team or individual in getting practice right is to get the game right, and we do that through analysis of who and what wins the games we set out to play.

Analyze the Game

- Use data to pick out the top performers.
- Observe and analyze performance data to discern what skills top performers have in common.
- Analyze and describe those skills in terms that provide a clear map to others who want to replicate them.

RULE 10
ISOLATE THE SKILL

Heart surgery is complex. It takes several years to learn. So where do you begin? While it is important to provide a context for medical students to get an overview, the real learning, the real practice begins with one skill and then another done over and over again in isolation. What do we mean by isolation? Consider suturing, one of the many steps in heart surgery. Suturing is complex in itself and must be further broken down. The novice needs to know how to hold the surgical instrument, how to make the knots, how to close wounds, how to suture through scar tissue, how to select suture materials, and how to suture when drains and tubes are needed. Before she can try this out in the real-world setting of surgery, she has many hours of practicing knots on oranges and suturing tubes to cadavers ahead of her. This is the central notion of Rule 10: having identified each skill or technique you need to build in your performers, you begin by teaching and practicing those skills in their simplest form and by breaking the unit of learning and practice down into bite-sized chunks.

The ultimate objective is still to successfully use your new skills and others in an integrated setting—in the big game, in a surgery, or in a reading lesson. Practicing the technique in isolation, in a simplified setting, is ironically often the necessary first step to achieving that objective. This is what we described in the first chapter as a drill. But we caution that drills have to be carefully designed to meet the objectives you set forth in practice. Not all drills isolate skills. In your process of planning, be sure to design the drill that isolates first. (We will look at ways to add complexity in Rule 12.)

To better understand what an isolated-skill drill could look like, let's see an example from our training workshops at Uncommon. For teachers to better implement the technique we call "100%," we knew we had to teach them to effectively use nonverbal hand gestures. So we developed a special drill. First we give teachers a list of student behaviors they might see in a typical class (for example, students putting their head down or their hand up at an inappropriate time, looking out the window, or fooling with their shoe). The teachers each design two or three hand gestures they could use to let the student know what behavior they would like to see in that moment (for example, pointing their finger toward their eyes and then toward the person speaking to remind students to look at the speaker; lowering their right hand from high to low in the air to signal putting their hand down; or folding their hands and straightening their back to show the posture they would like to see). In order to effectively isolate this particular skill, we have teachers practice implementing these new hand gestures by asking them to teach something they know well—a nursery rhyme or the Pledge of Allegiance—while pre-designated participants demonstrate the problematic student behaviors. The teachers must use the hand signals to correct behavior while not breaking the flow of their teaching.

We also remove other complications of the classroom setting in several ways. Most students comply entirely with a teacher's lesson, eliminating the need to scan and monitor the majority of students. We make noncompliance planned and predictable—the teacher knows what the behavior will be and whom it will be coming from—and we even ask the participants to make the behavior visually exaggerated so that teachers can easily identify it. We simplify the lesson plan and do not spend any time discussing how well they taught the lesson to the class. And we take away the pressure of pacing: with the guarantee of student compliance and engagement, the teachers do not need to go faster than they can comfortably practice the hand signals.

The teachers use their hand signals several times over the course of this exercise with the goal that the signals become more and more natural to them, ideally creating an inextricable link to the behavioral expectations they will reinforce every day. Teachers will be much more likely to use this form of intervention when appropriate in their classroom, sometimes without even being aware that they are using it, because they have practiced it. They become more comfortable with the skill in isolation and ideally enter it into muscle memory.

Now let's meet Tony, a manager who has just brought on a new sales team with high hopes of outselling every other sales team in the company. Tony wants to get them out there selling as soon as possible, so he gives them all the information they need to know and then has them practice multiple skills at one time: cold-calling clients and running sales meetings. They all participate eagerly, happy to practice the skills they will need for success. Tony sees that right away everyone is getting better, and that some of the new hires have strong technique already, so he sends them out to begin selling. The early results are poor: sales are low and so is morale. Tony again observes his team and realizes that they are all over the map. The ones who are not doing well are missing some of the basic skills of eye contact and listening. Some of the successful ones are missing some of the basic skills as well, but have figured out ways to compensate. A couple of them have not mastered what the bottom line for clients would be, nor are they able to communicate about it. Others are good at providing the bottom line but are not listening to their clients. The team is spending their time on the equivalent of writing while holding the pencil the wrong way, or practicing sutures while holding the needle incorrectly. They are inscribing poor technique by using it again and again, and getting by. Tony knows that at some point they will plateau unless he goes back and retrains them with these basic skills.

This situation can easily unfold in performance professions. The unfortunate norm is to bring new people into a company and expect them to perform regardless of the degree to which they have developed individual skills. In on-boarding new employees, trainers rarely ask them to practice discrete skills in isolation. In the best scenarios, professionals go back and develop those skills as necessary. More often, though, they try to get by with compensation skills. You eventually hire others to mask their weaknesses, or you work around the skills they never developed. Far better is to consider preparation programs as an opportunity to break down performance and ensure a strong foundation.

Isolate the Skill

- When teaching a technique or skill, practice the skill in isolation until the learner has mastered it.
- Uncover and retrain when compensatory skills are masking the need for isolated skill development.

LEARNINGS: CATNIP

When his teams first practiced shooting or dribbling, John Wooden often made his players work *without* the ball. "One of the challenges I faced during practice," he wrote in *Wooden on Leadership*, "was the distraction caused by a player's natural instinct and desire to score baskets or grab rebounds. Either urge is such a powerful siren song that it's hard to make them pay attention and learn the 'dull' fundamentals that ensure success in scoring and rebounding—such things as pivoting, hand and arm movement, and routes on play." Wooden called the seductive draw of the things that recall the drama of performance too directly or intensely "catnip," because they can drive participants to distraction. While our instincts often tell us to recreate those situations to make practice more useful, he tried to remove them during the learning process.

RULE 11
NAME IT

Every start-up company (and every new parent) is well aware of the importance of naming. When it comes to branding a new company, people willingly spend hours of time and often considerable amounts of money on finding the perfect name. You select the names that show exactly who you are and who you aren't, names that inspire your staff to strive for greatness and that hook people in to exactly what you offer. You avoid the bland, the overused, the gimmicky. You do this because your name sets the course for your company, and as it grows and changes, you hope your name will continue to represent the outstanding company you established.

While you clearly understand the power of a name, you often neglect this important rule when it comes to developing your team. You have an opportunity to name the skills you use each day, to create your own shorthand for the skills that matter the most. If done thoughtfully, giving the skills you are working on and the drills you use to practice them meaningful names can be a powerful tool, indeed too powerful to dismiss or ignore.

Naming the skills you aim to practice in isolation creates a language for your team. Given that these skills of high performance are exactly what you want your staff to spend their time talking about and focusing on, ideally their names will be logical and memorable. Not only that, but the best names will continue to shape the skills. The technique name "100%" is much more powerful and absolute than if Doug had named the technique, say, "Everybody." Each time we use "100%" to discuss the technique, the name signals and reinforces the muscularity of the technique in a way that "Everybody" never would. Identifying skills is a prerequisite to naming, but it does not guarantee an apt name. Likewise, simply naming techniques without surfacing the discrete skills will not provide the clarity people need to improve.

It's the combination of identifying and naming skills that makes the design of practice effective. A set of names for essential techniques becomes a powerful shorthand for talent development. It becomes a highly efficient management tool as well, conserving one of the most precious resources you can never get enough of: time. With this common language comes an efficiency which creates greater capacity to develop more talent.

Sometimes the best names come in spontaneous moments of practice, but often the best are those you have chosen carefully. You don't want to create more profession-specific names to make people feel like insiders who use a special language, to give the appearance of complexity to otherwise simple and straightforward aspects of performance, or to sound clever. There is a vast difference between names that build, sustain, and even amplify meaning, and jargon, which the more it gets used, the more vague and lifeless it becomes. You want to avoid the pitfalls of jargon, which can be nonspecific language that replaces and obscures otherwise perfectly clear messages (for example, "Let's put our heads together" could simply mean "Meet with me," or you may really mean "Figure it out"). Or, words can lose meaning when terms are misused and the original concept is diluted (such as with the term "synergy"). To avoid these traps, the descriptions of the techniques have to be specific, the names have to be meaningful and clear, and the use of the names has to be monitored and reinforced to ensure that terms are used consistently.

The power of naming goes even further. When school leaders have become fluent in the techniques from *Teach Like a Champion* and use them regularly to discuss teacher performance, this taxonomy of skills becomes a framework and influences the way we see and analyze teacher performance. In debriefing lessons with teacher candidates, our school leaders invariably reference these techniques because we analyze teacher performance according to that framework.

Invest the time in creating powerful names for the skills that are important. Then, as you develop people, use these names so that they don't collect dust on a shelf. Insist that people use the names when discussing performance, an idea we will pick up again in the sixth chapter, "Post Practice." And listen closely that your team consistently uses the names to refer to what you are referring to, and correct the team when there is misalignment. You will preserve the hard work of crafting the best names by ensuring they don't mean different things to different people. This will also preserve the names' power to shape practice.

Name It

- Name each skill or technique you have identified as an important building block for outstanding performance.
- Monitor the use of this shared vocabulary: use the names, ask staff to use them, and then ensure that the names are being used correctly.

RULE 12
INTEGRATE THE SKILLS

After breaking down performance and practicing discrete skills, it's time to scale the complexity of the practice back up and begin to integrate the skills into authentic contexts. This does not mean that you should turn immediately to the scrimmage (the limitations of the scrimmage were laid out in Rule 7). When you begin to integrate skills and make the practice look more authentic, a variety of drills is still the most effective way to practice. As you begin practicing skills in combinations that more closely resemble the game, you need to attend to three aspects of practice: (1) practicing skills in game-like scenarios, (2) applying the skill of "matching" the right techniques to the right moments, and (3) putting practice into the game environment.

Game-like Scenarios

Manchester United coach Rene Meulensteen has a video on the website FourFourTwo.com about improving technique. He observes that most teams use a "one v. one drill,"[4] with one player in possession of the ball and the other player charging straight at him, attempting to take it away. They do this to practice the basic skill of maintaining possession of the ball, but he argues that that is not enough. You need to practice "one v. one" drills with a defender coming from the side, from behind you, and from an angle in front, all possible (and we'd argue more likely) scenarios you would see in the game. This is the overlap between isolation and integration: you have to master the basic skill (maintaining possession of the ball) in a variety of realistic settings, or you haven't really mastered the skill. Most people assume that practicing with the defender coming straight in covers the development of that skill, but it doesn't. It prepares players to perform in the situation they will be least likely to face in the game.[5]

We took this lesson to heart when creating a practice drill for "No Opt Out," a technique that describes the way teachers respond to students so as not to let them off the hook for answering a question. It starts simply with the practice of a basic scripted sequence. Then we changed it slightly to include times when students don't give the answer because they are shy or are refusing to answer. We changed it again so that the student who provided the answer in the first and second rounds doesn't get it in the third. In this drill, teachers are preparing not only to use No Opt Out, but to use it nimbly in all the ways they might need to use it in the big game.

Matching

A story from a summer professional development session at one of our Uncommon schools illustrates the idea of matching. The workshop was designed to introduce teachers to the technique "100%." A rookie teacher had done the first activity for nonverbal corrections, practicing her hand gestures. She was doing well. Next, the practice switched to integrating "100%" into a role play that more closely resembled a typical class. The teacher was to practice her procedure for lining up students to leave class, using the teachers in the workshop as her "students." The goal was to line up the students while quickly and successfully correcting off-task behaviors. Again, the skill she had just practiced was correcting student behavior with gestures while continuing to teach. But suddenly, in this role play, she was confronted with off-task behavior from two students while she was not in the middle of teaching. The whole "class" watched as she stood in the front of the room and awkwardly paused, trying to get students' attention so that she could use her very best gestures. What she and others now realized was that that wasn't the right intervention for that moment. She needed to give a lightning-quick verbal correction, either anonymously ("I still need one; you know who you are") or a lightning-quick correction ("I need Josh, but I have Ethan"), and then move on. Instead, her least invasive intervention turned out to be much more invasive than other corrections would be. Why didn't she pull out the other interventions?

While this teacher demonstrated that she was prepared to use the skill she had developed in isolated practice, and she might have been ready to integrate that skill into a more authentic setting, she was not ready to integrate the whole repertoire of corrections. She was blindsided by this shift from the application of one skill to having to decide which skill to apply. On the surface it looked like the integrated practice was just adding the next layer of complexity. In fact, it was introducing a new skill, that of knowing which correction to use in which situation. We have to acknowledge that there is another skill to be built to ensure success: the skill of matching the right intervention or skill to the right moment. This skill, like the others, can be built through practice. The objective of a matching drill is to make the right decision about which move to use. Drills to practice matching fold two or three skills together and/or two or three situations together. This could mean you role-play a scenario several times: each time it starts the same, but then it takes a different direction requiring one of the moves in the newly built repertoire. Each iteration requires reflection and feedback on whether you made the right choice, so that you intentionally develop the decision making skills so that they will become instinctual.

Game Environment

When crafting your practice to resemble reality, the goal is that by making the practice look and feel closer and closer to true performance, the skills will transfer over during performance; the instinct you have built in practice will kick in. Another way to ensure that practice "resembles reality" is to attend to the practice environment. "State-dependent learning" is the idea that your ability to learn and retain information is affected by some element of your state of being. One element would be your environment; that is, you do better on a test when you take it in the same room you learned in. (Doug used to put this research into action in college by studying for exams in the rooms where he would take them.) Applying this to practice, the closer the practice environment is to the performance environment, the more likely people will replicate their success in performance.

Consider the design of the skills center at Weill Cornell Medical College. It is specifically engineered to create realistic scenarios in which residents and attending physicians can practice in the clinical setting without risk of injury to the patient or damage to the patient relationship. This environment is as similar as possible to the rooms of the hospital, and as such the practice spaces are outfitted identically to the real thing: the same beds, the same tools, even the same wall color are used in the simulation room. The college makes this level of investment in its practice space because it yields results and helps doctors apply their learning when they are in actual hospital rooms.

While integrating skills in more authentic contexts, teachers can get more from practice if they stand up and use the formal pose they will use with their students. It is even more helpful if the room is set up as their classroom and they can move around as they will when actually teaching. Practicing in their actual classroom is even better. All of this will leave teachers with the memory of being successful, of being the teacher they want to be in the big game.

Integrate the Skills

- After teaching discrete skills, create practice that places the skills in situations participants could face in the game.
- Create practice that helps people learn to match the right skills to the right situations.
- Consider simulating the performance environment to ensure that successful practice translates to successful performance.

RULE 13
MAKE A PLAN

No one would argue the notion that you need to plan out your practices. Coaches, managers, organizational development teams all plan for the time they have to develop their staff. Agendas are made, slide decks are polished, and discussion topics are wordsmithed. But what makes a good plan? What details should you attend to in the planning process to ensure it is effective? As we have learned from our work at Uncommon over the past several years, chances are that what you are doing now probably isn't nearly good enough, if you want exceptional results from your practice sessions. Specifically, we are perpetually astonished at just how much it pays off to do three things: (1) plan with data-driven objectives in mind; (2) plan down to the last minute; and (3) rehearse and revise the plan. This may seem obvious. Once again, we'll take a big bite of humble pie and say that we, like most people, were initially reluctant to invest the time and energy into such planning. We will also exhort that when you do it, it is well worth it.

Plan with Data-Driven Objectives in Mind

In the previous chapter, we made a case for practicing with clear, measureable objectives, limiting the number of those objectives and knowing in concrete terms what it looks like when an objective is met. Having that mindset will dramatically alter practice for many of us, but it still leaves the question of how to identify what your team needs so that it can practice for the right objectives.

In the documentary *The Heart of the Game*, we find our answer. This documentary tells the story of Bill Resler, a tax professor at the University of Washington turned high school basketball coach. In the movie, you observe how Resler's bias towards numbers and spreadsheets translates into using video and data to improve the performance of the Roosevelt High School girls' basketball team. Five years after Resler's first season, the Roosevelt High School Roughriders go on to win the state championship.

You watch Resler work late into the night analyzing game and practice tapes and data on the precise skills (for example, one-to-one defense, inbounds, passing, fast breaks) that each girl needs to work on. From this he determines the number of minutes that need to be spent on each discrete skill at practice, and which skills are most important to overall individual and team performance. Using these valuable statistics, he creates a practice plan that details which skills players will practice, for how long, and with which players. He sets the objectives first and then plans the particular drills he will need to meet those objectives.

Coaches and leaders often fail to recognize that planning practice must be a data-driven endeavor. What is more, the best coaches constantly adapt their practice in response to what they learn about the needs of their team from on-the-job performance and from the results of practice itself. As people succeed at tasks, you add complexity; as they struggle, you reduce it. This data-driven process works alongside the set of skills you have worked so hard to identify. You develop your list of skills that lead to top performance in your "scope and sequence," a generic document that captures the order in which you would logically roll out each skill, and the amount of time you would expect to spend on each skill. That document is invaluable in reminding you what your team needs to learn. But any document has to be flexible to accept revisions once the data tell you what your team really needs.

Plan Down to the Last Minute

Good plans for practice leave nothing to chance. There is no question of which drill will be inserted where, or who will get a chance to practice which skills. There is no midpractice poll of what favorite drill to do next, no free time earned for efficiency in completing activities. Plans that lead to successful practice account for each minute with useful activity.

At Uncommon Schools, we have begun to plan our practices with this level of detail. Paul Bambrick-Santoyo, managing director for the North Star Network, developed a planning process and template that has spread to all our networks: the "Living the Learning" template (detailed in his book *Leverage Leadership*). It asks planners to map out exactly the objective for each section of the practice, the types of activity they will use to achieve those outcomes, how many minutes each piece will take, and exactly what materials will be required. Some were initially resistant to this level of planning. It is time-consuming and requires presenters to plan precisely what they will say, how they will word each question, and what answers or ideas they hope each question will generate from the participants.

Yet, planning with this level of detail is the way you can know in advance just how you need to spend each minute of a workshop to ensure that the participants reach the objective. This is how you ensure that what you get out of practice (results, as your team grows and develops) is on scale with what you put into practice (the resource of your staff members' time).

Rehearse and Revise the Plan

Coaches who care about results don't just plan to the last detail; they actually go so far as to try out the plan, rehearse it, and revise it to make sure that the practice will be perfect. Take Mike Shanahan, coach of the Washington Redskins, who spends more time preparing for practice than actually practicing. When reporter Barry Svrluga followed Shanahan around last December, he observed, "Wednesday and Thursday practices are preceded by walk-throughs—rehearsals for what will happen in practice." The coaches have mapped out a script—sometimes 40 pages long—of the plays they intend to use. Then before the practice, they bring the whole team to rehearse the practice they have scripted, walking through to check that everyone knows where he needs to be and when, and to ensure that the plans on paper translate into the practice they are looking for on the field. Questions that might arise from translating the written script to the playing field are answered; explanations of the next steps or the next moves are made during this time. The team comes to practice ready to use each moment *doing*—improving and inscribing success rather than talking about what they are doing.[6]

The time you make to practice training activities in advance always results in a better practice because it leads to better plans. We have scrapped activities, drastically revised activities, simplified directions for clarity, and built on successful activities whenever we have put in the time to rehearse the activities in advance. Is this worth the time? Realistically, you are often battling the clock to get everything done, especially to complete the painstakingly detailed plan for each practice. Not every piece of practice can be worked through in this detail in advance. It is a question of investment. Even so, the more you embrace practice as something you do to improve, the better you will want to get at helping your team practice. One of the ways we have invested in getting better at leading practice is in videotaping our practice sessions—both one-on-one sessions and practice with groups of teachers. We then analyze our sessions and get and give feedback on how to improve at practicing. When we do find the time to invest in strengthening our practices through rehearsal and revision, it always yields positive results.

Make a Plan
- Plan with data-driven objectives in mind, and plan to adapt.
- Plan down to the last minute.
- Rehearse and revise the plan.
- Videotape and reflect on practice sessions.

RULE 14
MAKE EACH MINUTE MATTER

If you want to be a coach, go buy a whistle. We are speaking metaphorically here, though in some cases our guidance may be literal; you may in fact want to go get a real whistle. If so, when you start looking you'll have a hard time finding one. Whistles aren't cool. The guy at the sporting goods store will look at you like you just asked for a wooden racket and a pair of too-tight double knit polyester tennis shorts. What are you, some kind of relic? You aren't supposed to blow a whistle. You are supposed to say, "OK, guys, I need everyone's attention over here. Please stop what you're doing. Come on over. I want to talk about what just happened," and here you humanely begin to discuss one of your participants' mistakes (or successes) from practice.

Frankly, doing this is a disaster. Whether you are running a large ad sales training event with hundreds of participants, gathering a small group of managers together to practice how to conduct effective performance reviews, or coaching a church choir, these words can undermine the efficiency of your practice.

Speaking them aloud takes 10 to 15 seconds, assuming that everyone hears you the first time and feels accountable enough to come right over (which they will likely only do if they see everyone else doing it). You'll be lucky if you're talking about your teachable moment within 30 seconds. By this time the moment will essentially have been lost. You will have extended the feedback loop (see Rule 25) and eroded its effect. And more important, you will have wasted time.

Unfortunately, trying to get a room full of professionals gathered at a training to all come to attention isn't easy. They are our colleagues. They are adults, not children in a classroom. It feels uncomfortable hauling out the whistle. But we learned the hard way in our trainings at Uncommon that it was essential to do just that. At first, whenever we had people break into, say, small groups and then needed them to stop and gather together again in a whole group, we struggled. They wanted to keep talking. But we tried to be very respectful in our efforts to get everyone's attention, and so we let the minutes tick away while we waited for all to finish their thoughts. We knew we had to fix this problem and so we instituted a simple clap. The first time we tried it, we told people that when we clapped it meant we were asking them to break off their conversations. We knew they wouldn't want to, and we apologized. We were glad they had so much of value to talk about. But we wanted to honor their time and make the most of it. So we would ask them to come to order quickly.

Things went pretty well. We definitely saved a lot of time. But the clap wasn't perfect. People didn't always hear it or know whether it was deliberate. Over time we decided to improve our signal. Three quick claps in a row, it turns out, is distinctive enough that people tend to hear it and respond right away. Sometimes we add two short claps as a ten-second warning before the three claps. This lets people start winding down so the cutoff isn't quite so abrupt. Sometimes we have participants give a response clap to actively engage them in the process of coming back together. We use a clap cue every time we need to bring a room back to attention from small group work, and every time people hear it they do the same thing. This, in short, is our whistle, and it saves us literally hours of time.

The difference between a great practice session and a good one—and often the difference between a great organization and a good one—is established in systems like these that allow your productive work to be obsessively efficient. Without these systems, practice sessions are characterized by one thing above all others: the wasting of time.

Great organizations step in with whistles—clear, distinctive signals—to make people's practice as efficient as possible, even in professional settings and even with adults. This means signals not only for when to close out small group work but for when breaks will end, for example. (We've started putting an online timer up on the projection screen showing people how much of a 10-minute break remains so that our 10-minute breaks don't become 20-minute breaks.) It means letting people know how much time they'll have for an activity so they can plan to finish it on time. It means setting expectations for when and how people can and should ask questions; that is, whether they should hold questions until the end or feel free to interrupt you. (Hint: if you opt for the latter, be prepared to risk not getting through all of your material.)

How are you wasting time? What can you do differently? Below we describe typical ways that time gets wasted in different settings, and we offer preliminary ideas for using time more effectively.

MILLING AROUND

Time Waster: In between activities that require additional setup or discussion among leaders or coaches, participants stand around doing little or nothing.

Remedy: Ideally, better preparation will eliminate much of this, but some occurrences are inevitable. Try a "back-pocket activity," a high-value activity that you've previously practiced to mastery and that you've given a distinctive name to. Participants engage in it while you make final preparations.

Example: You teach your daughter's soccer team a drill in which players divide into groups of four and two-touch the ball to one another using both feet. You call this drill "Barcelona" after the great Spanish club team. When you realize your cones aren't set up for the next drill you say, "Three minutes of Barcelona in groups of four. Go!"

WAITING TIME

Time Waster: Participants spend more of their time waiting in line to practice than they do actually practicing.

Remedy: Subdivide into smaller groups or prepractice in minigroups Or give participants an active role while they are waiting to participate.

Example: Your managers are practicing responding to defensiveness from their direct reports. In groups of six they watch one manager role-play a difficult conversation with an "employee" and give feedback. But participants spend most of their time watching. You insert a prepractice where participants pair off and do two-minute mini—role plays on simple versions to "warm up."

LONG DIRECTIONS

Time Waster: Leaders or coaches spend too much time explaining the setup of several unique drills or activities.

(Continued)

Remedy: Design a drill and name it (naming it saves time reexplaining it later). Whenever possible, reuse the same basic drill with multiple variations to increase the ratio of practice to directions.

Example: You train new trial lawyers and have created a drill for your staff to practice making opening statements. You call it "Trial by Fire" because it is quick and pressured (but fun, of course), involving a combination of planning and in-the-moment responses. You can use it for opening statements and change the nature of the trial. You also adapt it for closing statements and questioning during trials. The lawyers know the drill: once you say "Trial by Fire," they jump to their feet and get started.

TOO LITTLE ATTENTIVENESS

Time Waster: Valuable practice time is lost because participants are having side conversations or players are bouncing balls.

Remedy: Teach your expectation from the outset. Explain the behaviors that you are looking to cue when you use your whistle, and reinforce those expectations.

Example: In a workshop, explain in the beginning the cue you will use to get everyone back. Express that you know that will mean cutting off some great conversations before they are complete but that it will save valuable time. When a group starts a side conversation, use a "self-interrupt" and cut your sentence off in the middle to cue that you need them to continue on with the practice.

TOO MUCH TIME ON DISCUSSION

Time Waster: Participants spend more of their time discussing, debating, or debriefing rather than practicing.

Remedy: Cut discussions short: when planning opportunities for discussion, plan for too little time rather than too much. Circulate during practice to ensure that participants don't get mired in talk.

Example: After a session of practicing a presentation, participants get exactly two minutes to discuss with a partner their main takeaways. The leader takes no more than two comments to share with the whole group before transitioning to the next practice activity.

SMALL MOMENTS ARE OVERLOOKED

Time Waster: Leaders and coaches miss the quick, casual opportunities to insert practice into the day-to-day.

Remedy: Change your mindset from thinking that practice is something that only happens formally in staff training or at assigned times. Each time you find yourself giving feedback on performance, consider if you can take the next moment to practice what you have just talked about.

Example: In a conversation with an employee about a recent sales call, you give a suggestion for how to handle it differently. You follow up with, "Let's run through how that would sound."

Finally, simply being alert to the fact that efficient use of time is the obsession of every great coach can help you be alert to the critical task of problem solving when inefficiencies happen. Sometimes the solution is as simple as "having enough balls at the ready." John Wooden's plans for a drill he used included not just where players would stand but how many would stand in each place *and* where the balls would be placed *and* how many balls would be in each location *and* whose responsibility it would be to chase balls for the group so that they were never short. Be creative. Be urgent. Efficiency matters.

Make Each Minute Matter

- Get a whistle—real or metaphorical—to conserve the resource of time.
- Identify the ways you inadvertently waste time and create remedies as soon as possible.
- Turn those remedies into routines.

These rules will get you started, but there are two big aspects of effective practice that we have not yet discussed: modeling and feedback. They are so important to making your practice powerful, and so complex on their own, that we spend the next two chapters on rules for using both as part of practice.

USING MODELING

In the quest to set up practice in the right way for your team, to start them off practicing success, you will find moments where the best way to teach a skill is to model that skill. Indeed, many of the seemingly simplest things defy description. Consider the simple act of following a recipe. Let's imagine James, a novice to baking, who one day decides he wants to bake a loaf of bread. He pulls out a cookbook and finds a recipe for bread and decides to give it a try. At first glance, the recipe seems simple enough. Measure three cups of flour. Check. Pour three tablespoons of warm water into a large bowl. Good so far. He follows each step, but before long, James finds himself at a loss. The recipe says, "Proof the yeast." Huh? How do you proof yeast? James reads ahead. The recipe calls for James to knead the dough but warns against kneading until the dough is tough and elastic. From this description, he feels pretty certain he could figure out how to get it wrong, but he is unsure what it would look like to knead to the point of perfection. The recipe calls for James to "let the dough sit and rise, then punch it down." They want me to punch it? Really? This is the moment when James realizes that the recipe will take him only so far; this endeavor calls for Julia Child herself.

What James needs is a model. The recipe, he realizes, might be a great guide for someone who knows what he is doing, who has already acquired the techniques, but for a novice, seeing someone execute the steps is essential. This is where the cooking show comes in. One reason cooking shows are so popular is because they provide that model. In every field, with every profession and performance you set out to master, there are skills and techniques that are either more easily and efficiently mastered through modeling, or nearly impossible to learn without it. Think about your areas of expertise and learning. What needs modeling? What would be impossible to teach without demonstrations? It could be kneading dough, threading a needle, dribbling a ball, answering a client phone call, or etching a microchip—you likely wouldn't want to teach these skills to people without *showing* them.

But modeling can backfire too. As a parent, coach, or manager, you are watched by those who look to you for guidance. It can be terrifying to realize that you may inadvertently be demonstrating all the wrong things. Back in the 1990s, NBA star Charles Barkley announced, "I am not a role model." But of course he was, just as you are when you accept a leadership role, when you are selected by your boss to train others, or when you launch your own team. The reality is that people will model their own actions, consciously or unconsciously, after the actions of their leader or coach. We have seen over and over the power of modeling in accelerating successful practice. The best developers of talent will harness this natural inclination to follow models and deliberately use it as a key part of practice to support the growth of their team. Knowing that they are being watched, they deliberately choose and shape their own actions to influence the group. They also realize the cost of not doing this. If they fail to give their staff explicit direction about the model to follow, the staff will still follow a default model, either consciously or not. In teaching, this means teachers will most likely teach in the way they were taught rather than the way that is most successful. The rules here focus on how to present a model as part of practice to show learners exactly what you want them to learn to do. A model articulates a goal, a performance to emulate. Modeling a small, discrete skill can help make the expectation for action crystal clear. Modeling a complex skill, or modeling several techniques at once, can show how all the discrete pieces will eventually blend together into proficient performance.

RULE 15
MODEL *AND* DESCRIBE

Part of teaching a technique well is to describe for learners in no uncertain terms what the skill involves, what it looks like, and how to do it. Modeling is showing them what all these things look like. When a well-crafted description and a model are used strategically in tandem, they can be a powerful way to help people learn. Consider the following example: Denise has just started her new job in the development department of a nonprofit. This is her first job out of college, and she is whip smart and ready to do whatever it takes to build her career and realize her ambitions. After a few weeks on the job, her boss gives her positive feedback and a new assignment: to make calls to potential donors to gauge their interest in the organization as well as begin cultivating them for future fundraising and informational events. The only time Denise has made anything resembling an outreach call was when she asked her grandparents to donate money to her walk-a-thon. In other words, she has no idea what she is doing.

If these calls don't go well, it will reflect poorly not only on Denise but also on her boss and most importantly on the organization. Luckily her boss realizes this and has wisely set up a time with Denise to practice with another colleague who is particularly good at these types of calls—we'll call her Helen. Denise could not be luckier: not only is Helen great at calls to investors; she is also great at structuring practice for developing talent. First she *describes*, breaking down the pieces of the call into an outline and providing sample language for each piece. She talks Denise through the outline, answering questions and explaining where the outline is flexible or inflexible—in other words, where Denise has some room for improvisation and where she has very little. Then Helen *models* a call for Denise: she calls another colleague, whom she has prepped on how to respond, and runs through the call with her. She also tapes it so that as she and Denise talk about it later, she can replay particular parts. As needed, she will go back through the model with Denise and talk more about what she did and why at each step of the call.

For the novice, the model alone wouldn't do. Denise, having high aptitude for this task, could listen to what Helen does and go off and probably do a pretty good job. But without the description, Helen would leave a lot to chance. Inevitably, as Denise strikes out on her own to make calls, she will need to go off script and improvise. It's the description that provides the critical decision-making parameters to ensure she makes good choices.

On the other hand, just providing Denise with the description leaves a lot of room for her to get a call wrong. She may strike a false or condescending tone, or awkwardly facilitate the conversation by not quite managing the transitions between segments. Helen has demonstrated that in a practice session, when teaching a new skill, leaders need to balance modeling and describing. Together they make a powerful combination.

Model **and** *Describe*
- Use modeling to help learners replicate, and use description to help them understand.
- Using modeling and description together ensures that learners can flexibly apply what they have learned.

RULE 16
CALL YOUR SHOTS

Many professions use some method of "shadowing" as part of their training or on-boarding process. We understand why. When you have highly skilled staff members, people who consistently demonstrate excellence in performance, you want to leverage that strength. You also want to be clear with your new staff about whom they should emulate. But shadowing can be one of the least effective ways of modeling what you want new recruits to learn. Why? Because all too often you neglect to do the one simple thing that would make for a great learning experience: you don't call your shots. Some versions of billiards require that before you take your shot, you announce which ball you are going to sink, and where: "3-ball in the corner pocket." In modeling, you should make your intentions transparent as well, taking the time to pre-view and to prepare learners for what they should be looking at and for. Your newest staff members are untrained not only in what they are able to do but also in what they are able to identify as skill in others. If you don't tell people what to look for, they can end up observing useless things. It is funny when it's your mother-in-law making random observations about football ("Why do they do that butt-slapping thing?") but less so when you are determined to close the achievement gap.

Let's say that Amir is the newest hire to join a sales team. He is bright and eager. His training includes shadowing the senior member of the sales team, Sarah. He first follows Sarah into a meeting with a new client. The client is clearly interested in their product, but they still need to negotiate the terms of the sale in order to seal the deal. Amir watches in amazement as Sarah proposes various figures and then falls silent. The client is not speaking, and neither is Sarah. The tension in the room is pal-pable, and Amir worries that perhaps he should leave—he has caught his new mentor on a bad day. By the end of the meeting, however, Sarah and the new client find mutually agreeable terms and sign a new deal. The client leaves and Amir awkwardly smiles and looks away. When Sarah immediately whisks Amir off to the next meeting, he feels deep relief at avoiding an awkward conversation with her about what he just saw.

He next follows Sarah into an important meeting with a big client. Sarah is friendly and clearly knows the client well. She remarks to the client on their long history working together and the ways their partnership has been fruitful but also challenging. She gives the client a sense of where the company is heading next, and voices her concerns that the client may not like the changes ahead. Amir watches as Sarah seems to respond to the needs of the client and demonstrate her best effort to come up with a mutually agreeable contract. He is relieved for her and for himself, believing that this was just how these meetings should go, and ready to provide Sarah with lots of specific, positive feedback. Sarah and the client end the meeting with big smiles and robust handshakes.

Afterwards, Sarah asks Amir what he thought about the two meetings. He first expresses sympathy for the trial Sarah had to endure at the first meeting, an awkward moment made public by his presence. He stops before saying more—he doesn't want to dwell on it. He turns the conversation to the second meeting. He effusively compliments Sarah on her engaging manner and her ability to keep the conversation focused on the negotiation at hand while still keeping the conversation professional and pleasant. Sarah looks at Amir apologetically. She realizes that he has completely missed what was actually happening in the two meetings.

From the perspective of the experienced salesperson, the first meeting went even better than she had anticipated: her negotiations resulted in a contract that would increase revenue to the company by a wider margin than she had hoped. Knowing that she can sometimes overtalk in these situations, she was purposeful in being silent and putting the responsibility on the client to respond. As for the second meeting, while appreciative of Amir's enthusiasm, Sarah points out that she didn't meet her objective. Going into the meeting, she knew that the right course of action was to end the contract with the client. Instead, she caved in to the client and changed the contract, knowing full well that the client would end up upset and looking for a new distributer in a few months. What Amir read as pleasantness, Sarah critiqued as her own inability in the meeting to give a direct message.

Now Amir realizes that he read the situations all wrong. Sarah realizes it too. Imagine if they hadn't had time to debrief and Sarah had left Amir to make his own sense of the day. He would have learned the wrong things by focusing on the wrong moments and misinterpreting the moments he saw. In hindsight, Sarah sees the pitfalls: the reason Amir was shadowing her is that he is brand-new to this work; it was unfair and unrealistic to believe he would know how to interpret what he saw.

Consider how this experience might have unfolded had Sarah previewed for Amir what to look for in these meetings. She might have said, "Amir, watch what I do with this client. Here is the price I am looking for them to agree to. There may be periods of silence while I wait for the client to respond—it could feel awkward—but if I jump in to end the silence, it usually means backing down on the price we are asking for. See if you can identify other techniques I use to this end." Now he knows what to look for, increasing the likelihood he will see it, while she can assess his aptitude by seeing what else he picks up on, given her specific prompt, "What else do I do to achieve my goal?"

The real danger in using modeling without calling your shots is that it could start the cycle of practice off incorrectly, with the learner practicing the wrong thing—something peripheral or even detrimental to success. Amir would have started on his own work with the wrong idea of job proficiency, and quite possibly would have done a worse job in client meetings because of the ways he misinterpreted the model. A soccer player might watch what a star player does with her feet but miss what she does with her eyes, thus missing out on the key to making the play so effective. Struggling teachers often ask to watch the masters in the hope that they will learn how to "do it right," shore up their own weaknesses, and see ways to tackle some of the challenges they have been facing. This sounds good, but the problem is that they don't know what to look for. They may focus on the posters in the classroom when they really need to focus on how the teacher gives directions. As the lesson progresses, there is almost never anyone there to identify and label the discrete techniques the teacher is using. Unless the teachers doing the observing have a highly developed ability to pick out technique and identify each of the teacher's deliberate moves, they will draw their own conclusions about what makes the model teacher successful. When you take even a few moments to call your shots, you turn what could be a negative experience into a powerful opportunity to learn from the best.

Call Your Shots

- Before you model, tell those for whom you are modeling what to look for.

LEARNINGS: E-MAIL YOUR SHOT

Hilary Lewis, the founding dean of students for Excellence Girls Charter School in Brooklyn, New York, provides us with an excellent example of deliberate modeling in which she calls her shot. In the following e-mail, she focuses staff on how she will deliberately use praise to further student engagement and learning in morning meetings over the course of the week. She lets them know what she will be modeling so that they can look for the new skill—the important technique they will all learn and practice this week—and not get distracted by other things she may do during this time.

Greetings EGCS Faculty,

I'm writing today to begin a discussion on the next Behavior Taxonomy skill that we will be learning about and practicing together.

Precise Praise

Precise Praise is the idea that positive reinforcement is a critical tool, but only if it is used strategically. This means that when we praise our scholars, we must choose intentionally. We must think first about what we want to praise our scholars for at EG. (For example, we don't want to praise students for walking in HALLS when it's an expectation of ours because it sends the message that following our expectations could be extraordinary.)

(Continued)

There are four principles to Precise Praise listed below.

1. Differentiate Acknowledgement from Praise
2. Positive Loud; Critical Quiet (i.e. making the good stuff visible)
3. Reinforcing Actions, Not Traits
4. Genuine Praise

We will all learn more about these principles during PD on January 22nd; but until then, please pay attention this week and next week during Community Meeting as I will attempt to model Precise Praise for the whole school.

As always—thank you for all of your hard work and dedication. I'm looking forward to working on this element of the Taxonomy with each of you.

Hilary

Ms. Lewis calls her shot by telling staff she will be deliberately using precise praise. She goes further to talk about a common trap of precise praise so that they can pick out another layer of sophistication in the model. Importantly, she is also modeling as a leader what she wants from her staff: humility ("I will attempt . . ."), excitement about the work ahead, and the notion that in order to get better, we need to practice.

RULE 17
MAKE MODELS BELIEVABLE

What learners are looking for in a model, in addition to guidance on the proper technique, is to be convinced it works. They want to see the beautiful loaf of bread emerge from the oven, or see the final price agreed upon after the negotiations, to understand not only how to perform the skill but what will happen if they do it right. When a novice violinist sees a model of how to hold a bow properly while playing a short piece of music, the clear strong sound of the music signals the results of using the proper technique. When we see a demonstration of a powerful teaching technique, we hope to observe that the result is 30 out of 30 students on task and learning. Even the most motivated among us have moments of doubt and need convincing. When your first loaf of bread emerges from the oven steaming hot and hard as a rock, you want to see that a beautiful loaf can emerge not just from a commercial-grade oven but also from a twenty-year-old relic like the one you bought at your neighbor's yard sale. Seeing is believing. When people see that a technique or skill actually works, it can take away the excuses they might make for not trying.

That's why we use a lot of video of outstanding teachers when teaching the techniques from *Teach Like a Champion.* Our hope is that showing the technique done expertly will not only convince participants of the impact the techniques can have on students, but it will also help teachers learn that technique as well. The key is not that the video has to be a flawless demonstration of a technique for it to be a valuable model; it has to be believable and authentic. If not, if there is any way for a teacher to poke holes in the technique—"Of course the teachers in the video are successful. There are two of them and only one of me!"—then the model is worthless. What we don't want is for teachers to leave the workshop feeling like the model was great but "would never *really* work for me."

Sometimes the doubt goes deeper. Practitioners want to see and believe that the technique being modeled will work in their exact context. If they don't believe, they may not ever try it. You can see this phenomenon on the television show *Nanny 911,* or shows like it. On *Nanny 911* the nanny comes in every week and uses the same techniques to create order in a disorderly household with previously unruly children. Presumably, the parents who participate in these interventions on national television have regularly watched the show. They have seen what the nanny does in other homes. So why haven't they learned from the model? Quite likely they have decided that their children are different. Their children are the ones who will not respond to these techniques. They sometimes profess they have tried *everything* and nothing works. In fact, some viewers buy in to this notion that there may be some children out there who finally bring the nanny down: each week the children's behavior is described in new alarming detail, convincing viewers to tune in because Nanny might just meet her match. And so, each week Nanny not only tells parents what they must do to support their children (Be consistent! Give time-outs! Be calm! Use a behavior chart!); she shows parents that these methods actually work by modeling the techniques with *their children*. Only then do they believe it.

One way to make models believable is to ensure that modeling takes place in a context as close as possible to the context in which learners will perform. If they see that a particular technique works with a company that looks like theirs, they will have a hard time devising a reason not to try it. If possible, model for them in their own context. We call this push-in modeling. Let's say you want to introduce a manager to a new meeting facilitation technique; nothing will be more persuasive than modeling with the manager's staff in a meeting. If we apply this to teaching, having a struggling teacher go to a great teacher's room is good modeling, but much more believable is having the great teacher teach the students of the struggling teacher. For the hold-outs and doubters, the ideal is to model exactly in their context—their classroom with their students. More important to learners is that they see themselves following suit than that the model itself is flawlessly executed. While capturing the perfect moment on video can open the door to learning, push-in modeling with a few bumps in it is often better.

Make Models Believable
- Model in a context that is as similar as possible to the one in which the learner must perform.
- In-person modeling is often more believable than models that are prepared on video.

RULE 18
TRY SUPERMODELING

When teaching a new language, teachers often conduct class in the language they are teaching and by so doing, double down on the learning time. Not only do students practice conjugating verbs and complete exercises in the text to improve vocabulary and sentence structure, but they are also immersed in the language. Students hear the language every day: how the teacher strings words together, uses verb tenses, asks and answers questions, and pronounces the words. While the objective of the lesson focuses on the skills laid out in the text, students can learn so much more when the lesson is taught in the target language by absorbing the modeling the teacher provides.

Similarly, every staff meeting or professional development workshop is an opportunity to create an immersion experience—to model the best practices you want your staff to use even when (and particularly when) those practices are not the objective of the workshop. Let's say the objective of your professional development is for your managers to learn effective ways to motivate direct reports to meet or exceed their sales targets. You know that you will model those motivational techniques for them before they practice each one. You will attend not only to the words but to the posture, eye contact, and tone—the delivery of those words. In "supermodeling," you will also model how to give feedback as you do that for each person during practice. You will model how to present to a group. You will model how to manage time in presentations with the use of your timer. These additional skills that you model are not skills you expect your managers to master from this session, but the more practitioners hear and see the language and conventions of success, the more they will become ingrained and habitual for them. A simple way to reinforce the skills you supermodel is to ask staff to reflect not only on the content you have delivered but also on what they can gain from *how* you have conducted the workshop.

While this seems like a fairly obvious point, when you get supermodeling wrong you can get the whole cycle of practice wrong. When working with your staff, you are modeling, and whenever possible you need to model exactly as you wish to see them do things, in the tone and at the pace you would want to see. Let's say you are modeling a presentation and you want the staff to focus only on the way you use the slide presentation you have created. Even though you have created a focus for them (calling your shot), you are still modeling overall expectations for a quality presentation. As you model, you have a choice: to treat the time with adults as more informal and purely about the objectives of the specific demonstration, or to deliberately model your overall expectations for your staff. The strong likelihood is that when others apply your model, they will apply the tone and energy you modeled in addition to how you used slides. If you modeled in a casual way, they will no doubt practice in a casual way. The danger there is that people often perform in the big game in the way they have practiced, so monitoring the quality of your modeling is crucial.

Try Supermodeling

- Model in the way you want learners to perform.
- Model the skill you are teaching, but use teaching time also to model any other skills that you expect people to eventually learn.

RULE 19
INSIST THEY "WALK *THIS* WAY"

The intuitive nature of imitation has become clear to us through our experiences as parents. When Katie was out to dinner one night with her then three-year-old daughter, her daughter starting gesturing in a way that she had never seen before. She was rubbing her brow, folding her arms, looking a bit distressed and considerably older than three. After a few seconds, Katie realized that her daughter was directly imitating the gestures she observed in the man sitting at the next table—it was unmistakable. As he shifted his gestures, she followed his model, carefully studying him. Katie and her husband had a little laugh and then tried to distract their daughter for fear this imitation would offend the gentleman.

What happens to the intuitive nature of imitation as you get older? There's a classic moment in the film *Young Frankenstein* when Marty Feldman, playing Igor, beckons Dr. Frankenstein, played by Gene Wilder, to "Walk this way." When Dr. Frankenstein simply follows along behind him, Igor, hunched over and limping with the aid of a small cane, hands him the cane and says, "*This* way!" and pantomimes walking with the cane until Dr. Frankenstein is also hunched and limping along. When Wilder starts imitating Feldman, it is a perfectly silly moment in part because of the physical humor, and in part because of the surprise and even levity you experience when someone closely imitates. This kind of imitation comes naturally. As Katie and her husband realized after dinner with their daughter, her imitation wasn't an isolated event. That in this instance their daughter had imitated gestures which were so unfamiliar called attention to something that she in fact did all the time: exactly imitate the ways she saw others acting. But at some point you train people out of it. You place a higher value on originality, and devalue copying. Yet, sometimes the best way to benefit from a model and practice and learn a new skill is truly to walk *this* way.

Consider the recent experience of one of the teacher leaders at Uncommon who was working with a struggling teacher. The teacher, we'll call her Rosie, was challenged by basic classroom management, and in particular was often creating more behavior issues as she slowed or stopped her lesson to correct students. Her coach had tried many interventions with her, and finally decided to teach Rosie's class while she observed. He reported that after she watched the demonstration, and they debriefed the modeling she had seen, Rosie seemed to get it. She saw that he had created nonverbal gestures for correcting students while continuing to teach. She heard him make very quick corrections of students as he then returned to the text. So he was stunned the next day when she was struggling as much as before. She was using nonverbal signals that weren't intuitive to students, so they didn't know how to comply. She was creating corrections that were quick but not clear, and they were negative, so again students didn't know how to follow the directions and didn't want to. Rosie had analyzed the model, but she got the application wrong.

You can easily overlook the notion that novices can and should apply a model by *directly imitating* it. It might seem obvious to some, but when presented with a model, most people feel they are supposed to put their own spin on it. We are often uncomfortable with this kind of imitation, which, when we were infants and toddlers, came so naturally. Indeed, it is the impulse to imitate that is responsible for our being the learning machines we are in the first years of our lives. But as adults, some people overintellectualize. They try to think through whether the model matches their style or their personality, and they get stuck there, not ever applying it. Some learners misapply the model in an attempt to give it their own spin, and then mistakenly assume it was the technique that didn't work for them rather than their implementation of the technique.

Learners need to hear that direct replication of the model is a completely legitimate way to approach a technique. When skills are clearly technical in nature—such as putting in a central line or replacing a motherboard—learners are much more apt to do exactly as their teachers do. You need to convince learners that even the seemingly soft skills of presentation and human interaction that are at play in so many professions can be learned more readily if you treat them as technical skills. You might assume that it squashes practitioners' freedom and creativity to tell them that what you expect is for them to copy the model you present.

In fact, it can free them to do simply as they see, to think less and act more, to feel the success of a simple moment, and it can ensure a proficient performance—the predecessor to creativity.

Insist They "Walk This Way"
- When asking people to follow a model, a useful first step is for them to imitate the model exactly.

RULE 20
MODEL SKINNY PARTS

Katie recently spent some time teaching her daughter, Aliza, to tie her shoes. She blocked off a chunk of time, and they sat down with one shoe and a clear goal. Katie started by modeling the whole tying process. She tied the shoe a couple of times, taking her time and trying to use exaggerated motions so there was nothing too subtle. She talked Aliza through it as she went. She was sure this would lead to shoe-tying success. Then Katie had Aliza try it. But Aliza couldn't even remember where to start. She didn't even know how to hold the laces—which hand? Katie quickly realized she had modeled too many steps, too quickly. So she slowed down and modeled each step. She showed her how to hold the laces, then watched her try it. She showed her how to form the first loop and which hand to hold it in. Aliza's turn. Then the big loop-around move. Katie modeled that one again and again, because it was the trickiest part. She had to model small chunks for Aliza until she could do those small pieces. She made up phrases for each piece she was modeling so she could reinforce when it was Aliza's turn to try it out. Then they could go on to the next part. After a time, they could put all the steps together. When Aliza forgot, Katie modeled again, and when she got it, Katie backed off. Then Aliza tied them with Katie just cuing her with the phrases. Finally, she could do it without any guidance at all.

You might make the mistake that Katie originally made all the time in professional settings, but unlike Katie's daughter, who willingly admitted she didn't get it, your employees usually work hard to cover up for the fact that they are lost. You show them how to do a presentation, how to use various programs or analyze data, moving quickly through your modeling. You often speed along because you don't want to insult your new hire's intelligence. Usually, you have lost sight of the learner's perspective and you've forgotten how complex the task is for a novice. You model too much and then cheerfully ask if there are any questions. Your new, eager employee, out to prove his competence, smiles and says, "No. I am all set. When would you like me to send this to you?" He walks away and immediately breaks into a sweat trying to figure out what he should do first.

In the second chapter we made a case for teaching skills in isolation, for breaking down the learning into manageable parts so learners can focus on one skill at a time. That is in part the issue here—not trying to learn and practice overly complex skills too soon. But while Katie's daughter could do most of the small skills related to shoe tying, modeling skinny parts helped her to build the connections between skills and to sequence them by following along a clear, deliberate modeling of the progression of the parts.

Modeling "skinny parts" of skills or techniques takes time, but it pays off tremendously in terms of successful practice and performance and the eventual time it takes the novice to learn the new skills. If the learner is struggling in her practice of a new skill, model a skinnier part, as small as it needs to be, and add to it only when she is ready.

One way we model skinny parts for staff is by playing "Copy Cat." This form of micromodeling can be applied when you are teaming up on a performance—teaching a class, running a meeting, or making a presentation. The expert models something and then gives the novice the chance to try it. They go back and forth until the novice picks it up. The expert can emphasize different aspects each time to cue the novice on how to adjust his practice when it is again his turn. In this form of in-the-moment modeling, the practice is more successful not only because we model smaller chunks but also because learners are practicing concurrently with the modeling.

Model Skinny Parts

- Model complex skills one step at a time and repeat when necessary.
- Play a game of "Copy Cat" with learners to model small skills until mastery and then build on that.

RULE 21
MODEL THE PATH

In some cases, with some techniques, for modeling to lead to successful practice, novices need a model not only of proficient performance but also of the steps that experts have taken to get there. Let's say you are a highly successful soccer coach and today you are modeling for a young, up-and-coming coach what you see as key to your success: how you coach *during* the game. He watches you as you draw diagrams, take notes, and have a few small side conversations as players come out. He sees that occasionally you call out to specific players in short, one-or-two-word commands. He watches you do very little, in fact, because that is one of the keys: you pull back during games, knowing that you have taught the team what they need to know in advance. While this is important for the new coach to see, it alone doesn't show him how to coach during a game. What is not obvious from that modeling is how you developed your team such that your way of coaching works. What is missing are the ways you put those short commands into place so that they could trigger complex action from the team. If the new coach were to just apply what he saw during this game on his own team, they would likely receive no guidance because he would have missed all the hard work and intentional steps that led to this successful coaching.

One of the keys to the success of all the Uncommon schools is the development of strong classroom systems and routines. As we thought about how to train people in creating and maintaining systems and routines, we started where we often start, by scanning hours of video of the best teachers for great examples of the technique. One of the golden moments we found was of Shadell Noel, a founding kindergarten teacher at North Star Academy Elementary School. In the video she greets each of the 30 kindergarteners one at a time, shaking their hands at the doorway. The camera turns into the room, and what we see are those 30 five- and six-year-olds sitting up straight at their desks, hands folded. Ms. Noel walks to the front of the room, and the students do their college cheer in perfect unison. Within seconds they are standing up, and filing in line over to the carpet. Instruction begins right away. It takes your breath away: the children are happy and smiling, the classroom orderly and calm, and not a second is wasted. This is the power of routines.

We also realized the risk involved in showing this clip to teach novices about systems and routines. If you have spent much time with kindergarten-aged children, you will be stunned by the apparent magic Ms. Noel has worked in teaching them the systems and routines of her classroom. This video succeeds at modeling what we want the end result to look like, but it doesn't show how to get there—an equally important piece to model. We have some amazing teachers in our schools, and we have been fortunate enough to catch glimpses of their brilliance on video. Sometimes showing our novice teachers these videos has an unintended consequence of overwhelming them and making them feel further away from being great, rather than one step closer. They end up feeling that excellence is really magic rather than something they can achieve. Some of this can be minimized through how you frame the use of models. However, to the extent possible, the models you provide should demonstrate something replicable, or they should give the learner insight into where to start practicing.

One way to solve this is to present a model of major steps along the path to creating the end product. In other words, you can model both process as well as product. For the systems and routines example, we decided to capture video of teachers on the first day of class as they first taught their systems to their students, and then again a month later once the systems were more routinized but still not complete. Another solution is to model something imperfectly, and then model taking and applying feedback to improve. This can relieve the pressure of trying to be close to perfect on beginning practice and can still be controlled by the person modeling, who can choose where to make mistakes. Most learners will miss the mark in small ways as they begin to practice, and their ability to take and apply feedback will dictate whether they practice successfully.

Consider the applications for your area of expertise. If you are successful in sales, it is highly likely that you devote time and energy to building relationships with your clients, with potential clients, and even with unlikely customers. If you model sales meetings with current clients only, your new hires will miss out on all the hard work you put in leading up to that moment. They might watch you make inside jokes or strike a more casual tone with a particular client—you know the client so well and that the person doesn't require or respond to formality. If a new hire tried to apply that tone with a client without taking all the steps you had taken to build that relationship, chances are it would completely backfire, offend the client, and make the new guy look unprofessional.

When you become great at your job, you often make it look easy. While being a great achievement that supports you in doing the work for a long time, it can cause new hires to panic or doubt their ability because they can't just replicate what they see. Avoid this potential pitfall of modeling by carefully considering what steps you needed to take to build top performance in yourself, and then model that path for others.

Model the Path

* Model the process as well as the product to ensure that people have a clear picture of how to get to the end goal.

RULE 22
GET READY FOR YOUR CLOSE-UP

Modeling live, during practice, can be great. It allows for flexibility and spontaneity. But it can be disastrous as well. Humidity can make an instrument fall out of tune; rain can make the ball extra slippery; and the team you model with can throw curve balls you never predicted. When you want to control the message, the best way to provide strong models is by using video to demonstrate champion practitioners at work.

You can select and cut video to show exactly what you want and no more, culling out any footage that may dilute the power of the precise technique you are trying to highlight. Also, you can re-watch a model on a video as many times as you need to in order to break down, slow down, or repeat a technique to better learn it. You can focus practice on different pieces of the model in stages: what was said, how it was said, and what was communicated nonverbally. Rather than sending someone to watch another colleague model a skill or technique and hoping that the model goes according to your vision, you can have the learner watch a video which you know will show your precise model, and then ask him to report back to you. If he misses the point, you can together review the video to correct his observation or modify your own.

People use video in various ways to model as a launching pad to practice. We have compiled hours and hours of powerful models by filming our best teachers and then cutting up the video into 30-second segments showing techniques modeled particularly well. We have devoted a lot of time to this endeavor because it was worth it to us. The result of our use of video for modeling has meant the rapid spread of the best techniques to our team of highly competent teachers in our schools across three states. This has yielded more and more high-quality models, which we have again captured on video as the teachers have applied what they saw modeled in the first round and made even better. It also means we can now share models more easily: rather than traveling to a classroom in Boston or Rochester, we can watch videos posted on various sharing sites on the internet and have nearly immediate access to high-quality models for use in teaching the techniques to more teachers.

Every video need not be a masterpiece of editing to be helpful. If you don't have the time or expertise to work for quality, you can focus your efforts on quantity instead. This can mean that you have a camera at the ready to capture great models as they occur, can easily capture them on your computer, and then quickly turn them around to share with other staff—in a weekly staff meeting ("Look what Denise did this week; this is what we hope all our client meetings look like") or in e-mail ("Check out the first 20 seconds of this video; Denise implements the skill we learned last week. Send me your analysis of what works here by the end of the day on Friday. Nice work, Denise!").

Just by using modeling frequently to shape the learning of others, you will prompt more frequent and more precise con-versations about what the best performances look like. When you take the extra step to capture those moments on video, you are codifying for your organization, across all employees, and for the talent you have yet to hire and develop in your organization.

Get Ready for Your Close-up
- Use video as an easy way for you or others to capture models that you can analyze, use, and reuse.

■ ■ ■

When effective modeling is an integral part of practice, it multi-plies the effect of practice. We have seen teachers improve more and faster when the skills that can make them great are frequently modeled for them. For James, our novice baker, modeling is essential for every moment where technique is involved. Basing his practice on what has been modeled makes the difference between failure and success (brick or bread).

In the next chapter, we will add another essential component to practice that could help James even more: feedback. This would take James from watching a baking show to attending baking class, where the teacher models and then watches as James immediately applies the model, and then gives him feedback and has him do it again if needed. In the class, James has the recipe *and* the modeling *and* the chance to immediately apply the model in practice, with corrective feedback. The use of modeling in this combination can lead to rapid success and encourage the learner to continue to practice and, with all of these tools, develop.

FEEDBACK

O ne of the fastest ways to improve performance is to improve feedback. Consider the British home defense during World War II. The British military quickly came to rely on a group of "spotters" to identify incoming German air attacks. These spotters didn't scan the skies. Instead, they listened carefully as aircraft approached, using their familiarity with engine sounds to determine whether a distant thrumming was a squadron of homeward-bound RAF planes or a bomb-laden sortie of enemy aircraft homing in on London. Reliable spotters were in short supply, so it wasn't long before they were being urgently asked to train others. However, their first efforts at training ended in failure. They weren't sure they could identify what they were listening for, never mind describing it clearly and actionably to someone else.

As David Eagleman relates in *Incognito: The Secret Lives of the Brain*, the military arrived at a seemingly miraculous solution. Novices would stand next to an experienced spotter in some fog-shrouded field and listen for a telltale drone, hazarding a guess as to whether the plane was British or German. The spotters would respond as quickly as possible with a yes or a no. No discussion, no explanation—after all, they couldn't explain the differences—just feedback: you got it or you didn't. Though none of them could explain what they were hearing, the trainees, in time, became quite accurate. Feedback, it turns out, can shape behavior in ways that defy expectations—and even logic.

But feedback must fit the situation. If all of the skills we needed to learn were as cut-and-dried—if we only needed to become good at choosing between a right and a wrong answer—then it would be a simple matter. As it happens, applying feedback in complex situations is challenging. A fairly daunting list of things can undermine its effectiveness. Feedback can be too vague to be actionable. It can be specific and clear only to have recipients misunderstand it. We can know what feedback to give but not how to establish social norms that allow us to be constructively critical of someone. We can give excellent feedback but overwhelm people with too much of it. We can focus only on the downside and miss the opportunity to give feedback on what people are good at. We can wait too long to give it. And even when feedback is just right, we may fail to impress upon participants that we expect them to do something with it. In this chapter, we address all of these issues.

But first, let's allow our inner optimists to observe what an immense opportunity lies before those who engineer the giving and getting of feedback. Upping the quality of your feedback offers an immense competitive advantage to people and organizations. That's something Katie thought about over the first year of the elementary school she started. She had only enough funding to hire a music teacher or a visual arts teacher, so she had to choose one program or the other. She at first leaned towards visual arts: a simpler program in many ways, and students would see their bright, colorful artwork gracing the hallways at school. In the end Katie chose music, though, specifically because feedback loops are such an inherent part of music instruction. She believed a good music teacher would socialize students to implement feedback as a matter of habit, and that this, over time, would be among the most important things she could offer her students.

RULE 23
PRACTICE *USING* FEEDBACK
(NOT JUST GETTING IT)

People get feedback all the time. The kids on your Little League team get it. So do your direct reports, we hope. This means that they probably practice "taking" feedback quite a bit—they learn to get better at nodding with eye contact, making their tone free of defensiveness, and taking notes, even. Recipients may signal that they take feedback seriously, that they value it, but this does not necessarily mean that they *use* feedback. Nor does it make them better at employing feedback over time. In fact, the opposite may happen. People may practice ways of taking feedback that help them avoid doing anything about it.

The three of us have done this ourselves. We might make a show of busily writing down feedback a colleague gives us. The response shows that we appreciate it. There is earnest nodding, but in fact we may already know we will ignore the advice once we leave the room. Or we may intend to use it but end up losing sight of it amidst the wreckage of our tasks list. Or perhaps we try it briefly and tell ourselves we have made enough progress, or that the feedback wouldn't really work.

These responses are common: people rarely practice *using* feedback. Really it's just as likely that people get better over time at ignoring or deflecting it since *that's what they often practice doing*: "Well, I can't really do that." "Oh, thanks, but I've tried that." "Thanks, that's really helpful." (No action follows.)

Using feedback well is something that responds to practice. People get better at it by doing it. They learn how to adapt someone else's advice so it fits their own style, for example; or how to focus on two or three key ideas at a time, or to take the risk of trying something that at first will be quite hard.

Getting good at using feedback—being coachable—is a skill with far-reaching implications. When people use feedback and improve, and see themselves improve at things, they come to believe in practice and in using feedback. And they're more likely to remain on an upward developmental curve for another reason. As Joshua Foer describes in his study of memory, *Moonwalking with Einstein,* people often arrive at an "OK Plateau," a point at which they stop improving at something despite the fact that they continue to do it regularly. "The secret to improving at a skill is to retain some degree of conscious control over it while practicing," he notes, "to force oneself to stay out of autopilot." The process of intentionally implementing feedback is likely to keep people in a practice state of increased consciousness and thus steeper improvement.

Research continually finds that teachers don't like their professional development very much and don't think that it helps. The causation runs both ways: training doesn't help because people don't trust it, and people don't trust it because it doesn't help them very much. If you train people successfully and they feel themselves getting better, however, it's much more likely they will trust and commit to it.

One of the keys to getting people to use feedback is building a culture of tacit accountability—one where participants are expected and incentivized to use the feedback they're given. If you've just given a member of your staff feedback, don't ask her what she thought of it and whether it was helpful; ask her how it worked when she tried it, or how many times she tried it, or to publicly commit to a time and place when she'll try it. We took on this challenge in our own workshops recently. Typically, participants might do a role play where they are asked to "teach" a simulated lesson to a group of their peers sitting around a table and playing the role of "students." The teachers would attempt to use a technique on which we had trained them, in just a two- or three-minute lesson. At the end of their two or three minutes they would get feedback from their peers on how they did.

As we did these activities, we realized we needed to do multiple rounds of practice, to let people practice, struggle, get feedback, and then try again. But even after we did that, people often seemed unaware of how useful feedback from group members could be. They would struggle. Their peers would offer insight—often small, actionable things they could do to make their implementation miles better. And the "teachers" would smile and nod, and that's it. Just as often the valuable insight would drift off into the ether.

Over time we realized we needed to appoint participants to a second role, a "coach," whose job was to watch for one "positive," something the teacher had done well that she should try to do more of—and one "delta," something that could have been better or something different the teacher could have tried. We stopped the activity two minutes into the role play, and the teacher received her feedback; she could ask clarifying questions *only briefly* to make sure she understood, and then she would start over going back to the beginning and attempting to use the feedback right away.

One benefit of this structure was its implicit accountability: it was hard for teachers to ignore the feedback. For one thing, it was public. Six or seven people had heard them get it; they were explicitly asked to try it just a minute later. It would be egregious not to try it at all. Another benefit was that after the feedback, the role play went back to the beginning—it was a replay of the same situation, not a continuation of the role play in which the requisite situation may not have occurred. This made the opportunity to use the feedback a reliable event. A third benefit was that the coach got to see right away if his or her feedback was effective—and this was important too since we were training instructional leaders whose job was to give effective feedback.

We found that people were stunned by how well tiny adjustments worked and how significant the effect could be. The coach would tell them to flash a smile when they asked the question; to put their arms behind their back. Whether they at first agreed with the feedback or not, they tried it, and often, against their initial instincts, the feedback proved effective. The results were immediately apparent. By being nudged to use the feedback, they came to believe in it and that small changes could indeed make a very big difference.

We added this wrinkle to almost every role play we do. It became a purpose in itself: to socialize people to use feedback, to practice using feedback and let people see themselves succeeding at change. Practicing using feedback before they've had a chance to rationalize it away can produce a demonstrably different result—and make people believe in their own power to shape their world.

Since reengineering our training sessions so that teachers would practice *using* feedback, we've found ourselves applying the insight we've gained in other settings. One in particular is applicable to almost any organization: preparing a manager for an especially critical or difficult conversation. This is one of the most potentially effective—but generally untapped—applications of practice in the business world. It is a classic example of a case where organizations don't think that practice applies to them, as Chip and Dan Heath observe in their outstanding book *Switch*: "Business people think . . . [y]ou plan and then you execute. There's no 'learning stage' or 'practice stage' in the middle. From the business perspective, practice looks like poor execution."

Consider a manager, David, who has to have a critical conversation with an employee, Susan, who is talented and smart but sloppy on details and who tends to hear feedback as advice (*Here's something you might consider trying*) rather than guidance (*As your manager I am asking [or telling] you to do it this way*). Not only has this led to mistakes and poor performance, but it has increased the level of tension between Susan and David. He's frustrated with her and inclined not to renew her contract. He's planned a meeting to communicate the extent of his concerns to her and to explain— again, in his mind, but for the last time—exactly what the problem is. To prepare, David schedules a meeting with his boss, Laura, in which they'll practice the meeting and role-play. During these role plays, feedback is a constant. Let's say David begins by summarizing the points he wants to make. "Great," Laura might say, "I like points two and three especially, but point one is a bit indirect. Why don't you roll through your intro points and imagine I'm Susan. Try to lay it on the line from the outset. We owe her that." Let's assume here that David does a quick rehearsal and that he sounds too blunt.

Susan might stop him. "What if you tried something like: 'I have to tell you that I need for you to make decisive progress at changing some things or this will be our last meeting before we start talking about a transition out of the organization. I'm sorry to tell you that, because I believe so much in what you could bring to the team, but we are at that point." David would not say, "Thanks, good suggestion," and keep going with the review of his plan for the meeting. He would go back to the top and try again using Laura's suggestions. He would force himself to practice *using* the feedback.

As David rolls through his intro a second time, he doesn't like what he hears. He sounds too sticky sweet, not like himself, and therefore not really honest. He stops himself, pauses, and looks at Laura. He says, "Let me try that again. I just have to say it like me." And back to the top he goes. Interestingly, David has here internalized the process of using feedback. The interruption and the feedback are his own—a self-correction. He has learned, through practice, to make a habit out of stopping and applying feedback right away.

The value here is not just for David but for Laura as well. Managers and coaches often "fly blind"; that is, they give the best advice they have, but they really have no idea whether it has helped. One of the key benefits of quick, public use of feedback is that it lets managers and coaches reliably see their own feedback at work. Coaches then learn which feedback—and method of delivering feedback—works best.

One last benefit of causing people to practice using feedback: it is a team-building exercise. After all, David's meeting with Susan became a shared project for him and Laura. As his boss, she became deeply vested in its success and became a stakeholder in the ideas he used to shape it. This, over time, has a positive cultural effect on an organization. Giving feedback to one another and getting better together makes improvement a team sport, builds trust, and unlocks the knowledge often buried in an organization's people.

Practice Using *Feedback (Not Just Getting It)*

- *Using* feedback is a different skill from accepting it. Build a culture where people get better at using feedback by doing it a lot.
- Cause people to practice putting their feedback to use as quickly as possible—by sending them back to the front of the line, for example.
- Observing the use of feedback right away helps managers and coaches see whether their advice works.

RULE 24
APPLY FIRST, THEN REFLECT

In the meeting between David and Laura, David did one other thing that was both counterintuitive and indicative of good practice. He used feedback from Laura before he reflected on or discussed it. David might have reacted to Laura's feedback first, saying, "Well, I think Susan is likely to get emotional. I don't think I can be quite that direct," for example. Instead, he went back to the top, started over, and tried Laura's feedback, causing the ensuing discussion to be based not only on his reaction to the idea but on its application—whether it worked in action. This brings us to our second rule of feedback: apply it first and then reflect on it.

When feedback is given, it's often the starting point of a discussion. This in turn often crowds out action. One of the most productive things you can tell participants who want to reflect on your feedback is "OK, you might be right. Try it first and we'll see."

Let's say you are working with a peer, Marta, to practice performance reviews you both must give your direct reports in the upcoming weeks. You role-play the review you intend to give one employee, Carol. You begin by describing two or three of her strengths and then talk about two key areas where she could improve. As you finish, Marta says, "You know, I think that your praise sounded a little throwaway, like you were just giving it so you could get to the things you didn't like about Carol's work. Could you add some detail—describe some specific times when she really helped the team—to make it feel more heartfelt?"

Typically, Marta's comment might cause you to reflect on your relationship with Carol: "Thanks, I think I do that too often. I really appreciate everything Carol does, but I don't always give her specific examples." Or you might reflect on larger management issues: "You know, I'm always torn by that. I know I'm supposed to give positives first and then negatives, but really I just want to get to the issues that are most important. I think it sounds formulaic to always give two positives then two negatives." These conversations are interesting and probably useful, but they are less useful than the alternative, which is continued practice. In fact, many times when running a practice session we have found that participants unintentionally (or otherwise) use reflection and earnest conversation as a way to avoid practice.

In this case, it will be more helpful if you rerun the practice session incorporating Marta's feedback, and then reflect on whether it worked. Feedback, remember, is often counterintuitive or unexpected for the recipient—if it was intuitive, one could argue, participants would think of it themselves. So reflecting on the feedback before you've tried it is premature; it's the outcome you get that matters.

In short, the sequence that practice should generally follow is

1. Practice
2. Feedback
3. Do over (repractice using the feedback)
4. Possibly do this multiple times
5. Reflect

This is different from the sequence that most people are naturally inclined to follow:

1. Practice
2. Feedback
3. Reflect and discuss
4. Possibly do over

We're not saying there can never be *any* discussion after feedback. Surely there are cases where discussion is more important than continued practice. But be skeptical. Discussion very quickly becomes a compensatory strategy, and even when it isn't, there's limitless time afterwards for reflection. The minutes when we're all together for practice, however, are priceless.

During our workshops we often circulate through the room as people practice. Generally our participants are in groups of eight with perhaps 20 groups in the room, so there is significant opportunity for people to practice at different rates. As we circulate, we usually find a group engaged in a discussion. Often they will engage us: "We were just talking about what you would do if . . ." These conversations are probably immensely valuable—later on. Reflection, to us, comes at the end, so we try to respond with the phrase, "Whose turn is it?" Our point is that reflection will be *better* later on when it is informed by rounds of practice that are, in turn, shaped by feedback. So practice, get feedback, and apply it. Then you can reflect on how the feedback worked.

Apply First, Then Reflect

- Reflection, while often worthwhile, can become a barrier to further practice. Ask people to apply feedback first, then reflect on it.
- When participants apply feedback and then reflect, they have more data to use in reflecting on the value of the feedback.
- Try using the phrase "Whose turn is it?" to respond to an excess of discussion when more practice would be preferable.

RULE 25
SHORTEN THE FEEDBACK LOOP

In *Moonwalking with Einstein,* Joshua Foer discusses a curious data point from the annals of medicine. You'd think doctors would get better over time at the things they practice every day, but in many cases they do not. Take mammographers, for example, who get *less* accurate with experience. Why? Foer points out that after reading a typical mammogram and making a diagnosis, they experience a long delay in their feedback loop. They make the call and find out if they were right only weeks or months later. By then they've forgotten what made them decide and perhaps feel a bit less urgency about understanding the data points that led them to be right or wrong. They still care deeply about their patients, but the bright fresh eyes of the young mother whose screening they reviewed are perhaps less pressing upon their minds.

With feedback, it turns out, speed is critically important— maybe the single most important factor in determining its success. Remember the British spotters? One of the keys to that training was that the feedback came within seconds. The direct connection between action and response was so strong it could even overcome a "black box," a situation in which no one could describe what the solution looked like.

In behavioral change, it's clear that speed of consequence beats strength of consequence pretty much every time. If you want to change behavior—and changing behavior strategically and intentionally for the better is what practice is—then shorten the feedback loop. Give participants feedback *right away*. This will improve performance far faster than giving more extensive feedback later on, even, arguably, if the later feedback is better. Speed matters most.

John Wooden was notoriously obsessive about this. As one of his former players wrote, "He believed correction was wasted unless done immediately." As the minutes slipped by, the player's mind and body would forget the situation. Once he'd practiced doing it wrong, the window rapidly snapped shut and correction becomes useless. If you're designing training or practice, then, shorten the feedback loop whenever possible—make feedback fast and frequent. The best way to achieve this outcome is to plan for feedback to be a regular part of practice. Our colleague Rob Richard experienced this in a recent course he took to learn to ride a motorcycle. One mistake, even a mistake in practice, could be disastrous, and so, Rob told us, the course was designed for fast feedback. There were two coaches, one who demonstrated and explained and sent him through a short course marked with obstacles, and a second who stood waiting, every time he completed the course, to give him immediate feedback. The coaches could have given him more extensive feedback. They could have written it down so he could have a record of it and read it over again. Instead, Rob's instructors chose to give feedback to him right away and send him back onto the course for another time through. Experienced motorcyclists understand in a way that most automobile drivers don't the danger of technique going uncorrected, and Rob's instructors were waiting for him with feedback before he even took off his helmet.

Katie saw the benefits of this recently while leading practice at a school. She was training on a technique called "Cold Call," where teachers call on students regardless of whether their hands are in the air. The technique is a major muscle group of academic rigor in the classroom but can be intimidating for teachers who've never tried it. After explaining the technique, Katie asked a trainee to practice in front of his peers, with them acting as students. He was nervous and made a simple, correctable error (calling the names first and then asking them a question, rather than the other way around). The original plan was for him to practice for two minutes and then get feedback from Katie and his peers, but as it became clear that he was struggling, Katie decided to shorten the feedback loop.

As Katie paused the exercise, she was careful to be calm and natural—she wanted to normalize error (Rule 31) and signal that experiencing difficulty is even expected during practice. She told the teacher he was very close to getting it right, but that he should start over and make one very simple change. He should ask the question, pause, and then identify the student who should answer. "Take a minute, rehearse that a few times in your head, then give me a nod, and we'll go back to the top and try it again. You're going to do fine," she said.

Interestingly, Katie's intervention shortened the feedback *twice*. She cut off the exercise and gave the teacher feedback right away, as soon as he began to struggle, and sent him back to the beginning so he would practice using the feedback. But even before that she asked him to rehearse in his head. There were just a few short seconds between when he began to founder and when she was there to support, and just a few seconds before he started to apply the feedback.

The teacher did as Katie asked, even though he was nervous and perhaps not really sold on the feedback. As Chip and Dan Heath point out in *Switch*, people often assume that the size of a solution has to match the size of a problem. In reality, a small change can often fix what is—or feels like—a big problem. That was the case here, but if Katie had, say, let someone else try and thus allowed the memory of the failure to become deeply imprinted amidst private anguish at the back of the line, the problem might have grown bigger. Instead, the memory of failure was truncated and instantly replaced with success.

The difference, as the teacher tried again, was instantly recognizable. The teacher used the technique for a minute and was visibly pleased and happy, to the degree that his peers recognized it and spontaneously gave him high fives and cheers. This was not only a watershed moment for him personally; it made practice something he believed in.

Certainly there are cases where you might not want to step in as decisively and where you might want to let participants work through difficulties for longer. This might be the case if your participants were further along in the learning cycle and the focus was on preparation for real-world application, and where part of the purpose was to let people recognize and self-correct when their implementation needed adjustment. That is a very worthy and real type of practice where this rule might not apply as clearly. The point is that when you want to use feedback to reinforce something, a fast response is the most effective thing you can use to make that point. When your purpose is not to get someone to do more or less of something, for example, when your purpose is to practice adapting to setting and situation, you will be less likely to shorten the feedback loop as aggressively. But it's worth thinking about all the things we try to get people to do (or not do) in practice but where we allow for a significant time lag before we tell them about it. It's not much good to make a mistake in a meeting and find out about it in your performance review three months later!

Shorten the Feedback Loop
- Speed of consequence beats strength of consequence pretty much every time. Give feedback right away, even if it's imperfect.
- Remember that a simple and small change, implemented right away, can be more effective than a complex rewiring of a skill.

RULE 26
USE THE POWER OF POSITIVE

We often assume that feedback is a tool for repair. You give it to fix something. It's the vehicle for telling people what they did wrong and how they can do it better. But as we noted in Rule 6, Practice "Bright Spots", there is opportunity for those who can get past the assumption that the goal is always to fix the things that are wrong with us. Over the past few decades, a groundbreaking group of "positive" psychologists has emerged with a focus not on what goes wrong but on what goes right. People cope effectively and sometimes heroically with incredible difficulty: they overcome, endure, and thrive in the face of adversity. Positive psychologists seek to study and learn from such cases and apply the lessons so that more of us respond with energy and vigor in the face of challenge.

We don't denigrate the importance of identifying areas for improvement and productively getting after them. Any productive sequence of practice must eventually do that, probably sooner rather than later, but a fix-it model underrates the compelling "power of positive" to guide change and improvement. Author and consultant Marcus Buckingham, whose book *First Break All the Rules* has consistently been ranked among top business books since its publication in 1999, has been widely influential in messaging that organizations get further managing strengths than weaknesses. The assumption that "each person's greatest room for growth is his or her areas of greatest weakness" is often not correct, he observes. In fact people tend to improve most and fastest at things they are good at or by applying their existing talents in new settings. Focusing feedback on strengths can be at least as productive as focusing it on weaknesses. *If you do it right.*

The "if" here is a big one, because most of us tend to rely on what we think is the most productive form of positive feedback: praise. Saying, "You did that well. Great job!" is nice. It motivates and inspires people. But we tend to think that's it, that positive feedback motivates people by making them feel good. Ironically, that may be the weakest part of positive feedback. To transform positive feedback from a pleasant motivational tool to a major muscle group of improvement, consider adding three simple tools—a statement of identification, a statement of application, and a statement of replication.

Let's look at an example. You're in the backyard teaching your daughter, Danielle, to field ground balls. She's a motivated kid and wants to learn, but there's a lot to know about ground balls. Gotta move those feet and get behind the ball so you don't have to reach. Gotta get your backside down and your head up. Gotta start with your glove open and your wrist flexed. Gotta start with your glove on the ground. At first you're just motivating Danielle, so you hit her with plenty of positive feedback: "You did that well, Danielle! Keep it up!" But what *is* "that" exactly? Telling Danielle to keep "it" up would be much more productive if you also told her what "it" was. What if you reworked your original statement—"You did that well, Danielle! Keep it up!"—to include an "identification statement" to help her see what the "it" was:

"Good, Danielle. You moved your feet quickly and got behind the ball. Keep it up."

Note that the statement is specific. It describes an action that Danielle can replicate. Your statement praising her feet is better than a statement that merely tells her that she "hustled," since she still might be unclear as to what exactly "hustle" looks like and how she can make it happen again. In fact, Danielle has done a lot of things right, so you have choices. For example, it may be that you want to focus less on any one thing she is doing now and more on the practice she has put in. You can still strive for clear identification:

"Good, Danielle. You practiced all week, and now look at you!"

Now you are focusing Danielle less on what she did with her feet while the ball was bounding her way and more on what she'd done for days to prepare for this moment. Both were factors in her success. Which one you choose depends on which part of the universe you want to open to Danielle's eyes. Stressing hard work and its connection to results is not an insignificant factor since as a culture we are probably too inclined to attribute to natural ability what is really a result of hard work and practice. The direct connection between diligent effort and results is not in fact always clear to many people, so making the direct line between inputs and outcomes clear can be powerful.

So now Danielle knows what she did right. She can connect the idea with a replicable action. In a perfect world, her internal narrative would sound something like this: "Hey, it worked! I'm going to focus on trying to make quick small sideways steps every time. In fact I'm going to ask Dad for ten more ground balls right now so I can build muscle memory. I want to remember what it feels like to do it right!"

Unfortunately, Danielle's internal narrative may not include every single one of those statements. She may not know how to replicate a success, or that doing so is a crucial element of successful practice (and successful learning). You can help her with that process by making a "replication statement," such as one of the following:

"Good. You really got your feet behind the ball. Now try to do the same thing going to your left."

"Good. You really got your feet behind the ball. Let's do it a few more times so you can really remember what that feels like."

The first replication statement encourages Danielle to think about how she can repeat her hard-won success in new skills. The second helps her to see the next steps towards excellence at the skills she's working on. Different approaches, same principle.

After a few hours in the backyard, Danielle can range to her right like Derek Jeter. Meanwhile here's what Danielle's ideal internal narrative might sound like: "I think there's something to this footwork thing. I mean, if using quick sideways steps to get myself into position before the ball comes helps with ground balls, I can probably apply this trick to fly balls too. And come to think of it, when tennis season rolls around, I suspect I'll hit the ball better if I can replicate the small quick steps. This has been a great day! Later when I become famous, I promise to say lovely things about my parents in a variety of speeches and interviews."

Okay, this is unlikely, but you can help her see some of the connections we've idealized here with an "application statement" such as this:

"Good, Danielle. Ten in a row! You're doing so well, so let's work on a couple of other ways you could use a quick start and small steps."

This gets to the core of Buckingham's idea about managing people's strengths. When you realize someone on your team does something well, you should immediately start thinking about other ways to use and apply that talent productively.

With that in mind, let's leave Danielle's rapid progress behind for a moment and return to David, who was preparing with his manager, Laura, to put his concerns about his direct report, Susan, on the line in an unequivocal way. David and Laura conduct a run-through where the two of them trade ideas and strategies and try them out in mini—role plays. Practicing his approach, David suddenly gets in the zone. His tone is spot-on: respectful but firm. He expresses genuine empathy for Susan but helps her see the urgency of her part of the improvement equation. It's a home run.

It's an incredible opportunity for Laura to leverage using an application statement. "That's it! Right there," she might say. "The tone you have right now is what you want to lead with. But more than that, we know that Susan gets emotional and can try to goad you into being the bad guy. You know, like when she says, 'So everything I do is useless??' I want you to try really hard to get back to this tone when and if she goes there. And in fact I want to practice that for a few minutes. You take points two and three from your talking points, and I'll be Susan. I'm going to get defensive and try to ratchet things up. See if you can use the tone you just used to keep things on an even keel."

Now Susan has helped David identify his success and not only replicate it but apply it to another setting. If this meeting goes well, she might do more of it, suggesting, for example, other places where David might draw on the voice he developed during their run-through or, alternatively, suggesting that David prepare for an upcoming organization-wide briefing with the same methods he used to write his successful talking points for the Susan meeting.

With a little practice, statements that add this kind of power to positive feedback can help anyone developing new skills to apply successes more intentionally, more often, and in new settings. It can help people move from strength to strength. Positive feedback, then, does more than motivate. It helps people use practice more effectively to get better. The coaches, managers, and teachers who can harness it give themselves a true competitive advantage and give their players, staff, or students the lasting gifts of success and the awareness of what builds it.

Use the Power of Positive
- What people do right is as important in practice as what they do wrong.
- Help people use their successes in three ways:
  > With a statement of identification to help participants see what they did right more clearly

> With a statement of replication to help them do it again
> With a statement of application to help them see new
> settings in which to apply their skill

RULE 27
LIMIT YOURSELF

You want to be really good at tennis. Always have. Now you've come into a small inheritance, and so you've hired "Super Coach" to help. He arrives wearing a Bjorn Borg headband and a cerulean blue Rafael Nadal shirt—a steely-eyed mix of retro and up-to-date. He knows everything. If you can download his knowledge, you will be the player you have always dreamed of being. But a few minutes into your first session, everything is going wrong. "I am going to tell you one more time," he says, as you stand like a child at the base line. "There are nine things you must do to hit a forehand. Only nine." Still, as hard as you try, you can't remember them all, *even though he reminds you of them over and over.* You focus on getting your racket back early (#2), and he berates you for not being sideways to the net (#4). You do that, and your footwork (#3) comes under assault. You begin to think about your footwork, and he reminds you of the imperative of the follow-through (#7). "Idiot," you're pretty sure you hear him mutter as he bends to pick up the balls lining your side of the net.

Turns out, knowing what to do is a long way from doing it; in fact, knowledge can get in the way of learning when it isn't doled out in manageable pieces. This is Super Coach's problem: asking you to pay attention to nine things at once is all but impossible. But he is not alone; most people—the three of us included!—are inclined to give people too much feedback at once. When performers or employees or team members or children are trying to concentrate on more than one or two specific things at once, their attention becomes fractured and diluted. Ironically this can result in reduced performance.

One of the keys to coaching, then, is to develop the self-discipline to focus on fewer things. Though you clearly see 15 things wrong with your daughter's rendition of the "Moonlight Sonata," you tell her about only the two most important *and hold off on everything else.* This is especially difficult because it feels good to be the coach and to have so much to share. In the end, though, you have to choose between being an impressive boss—one who knows everything—and an effective boss: one who helps a team member focus on the few things he most needs to develop. Sharing everything is a fool's errand. If your game is going to improve, you are going to have to march right over and tell Super Coach as much.

In individual coaching situations, the challenge is to tame your inner expert, but in the workplace it also means rethinking how you structure feedback. How do experts in the workplace find the time to provide any kind of feedback, much less feedback that is carefully planned and prioritized? This is particularly problematic in education, where one of the most commonly heard tales of woe is the story of the principal who can never find time to talk with her teachers about teaching. Indeed, a recent study in Miami found that principals there spent about 8 percent of their time observing in classrooms.[1] Imagine a coach who spent 8 percent of her time watching her players in the game!

Understanding that feedback needs to be parceled out carefully and strategically, we took on the logistical challenge of making this happen in our own schools. Almost all our teachers get regular feedback, either from the principal or from a leadership team; every two or three weeks is typical, but for many teachers it's much more. The feedback is informal and supportive, delivered in small bursts right after class (to shorten the feedback loop) and focused on strengths as much as areas for improvement. It comes from a variety of peers and bosses. But as you might guess, this is not necessarily a recipe for prioritizing and limiting feed-back. Making feedback frequent, by having a sizeable group of possible coaches and experts involved, meant that teachers were at risk of getting deluged with input.

That's why we use a tool originally developed by our colleague Paul Bambrick-Santoyo (and described in his book *Leverage Leadership*) which tracks feedback on an organizational level. The idea is for the principal and the department and grade-level chairs, all of whom give feedback, to coordinate so that they agree on the two most important things a given teacher should be working on—strengths or weaknesses—and agree to give 90 percent of their feedback on those two things. It would be relatively simple to replicate this in almost any organization: to coordinate the goals of team members so that those who gave feedback focused on, rather than distracted from, the most important things.

Limit Yourself

- Limit the amount of feedback you give; people can focus on and use only a few things at a time.
- When people get feedback from multiple sources, use a tracker to ensure that what people hear is consistent and not overwhelming.

RULE 28
MAKE IT AN EVERYDAY THING

Doug McCurry is a legend among the people we work with. The leader of Achievement First Schools, he is responsible for more than a dozen schools that achieve outstanding results with students born to poverty. Principals and managers we work with like to quote one of his trademark phrases, often just before they give one another feedback. "I'm going to give you a gift," they say, "the gift of feedback." Though they sometimes use the phrase with a bit of tongue in cheek, it still prepares recipients for feedback and reminds them that it implies respect. "One of the most memorable things one of my bosses at Pepsi told me was that if you really care about somebody, you give them constructive feedback," echoes Maigread Eichten, principal at Eichten Consulting and a former beverage industry CEO, in a recent interview in the *New York Times*. "And if you don't care about somebody you only say positive things." Feedback is hard to give, and hard to craft well. But a bit of culture building can go a long way to making it feel like a gift.

To make this possible you have to frame specific language that people can call upon consistently to make it safe, natural, and easy to give and get feedback. Ironically, one of the most effective tools is so simple that people may overlook it: sentence starters. Erica recently tried sentence starters in a workshop with teams of teachers from more than 25 schools and organizations. It was a diverse group, representative of both new and established organizational cultures and, presumably, a mix of cultures where, in some, feedback was naturally given and, in others, feedback was not yet normalized. To make sure that all of these groups were able to give feedback effectively right then and there, she suggested they use two specific phrases to start their conversations:

"One thing I thought was really effective was   " and "What if you tried . . ."

Every time the sentence starter was used, it made implicit reference to the fact that everyone was deliberately giving feedback because it mattered so much, and using the "starters" to ensure that they did so effectively. The usual litany of apologies and introductory remarks became unnecessary.

Incidentally, Erica also added a feedback loop at the end of her session, where participants shared especially useful feedback they had gotten from other participants. Discussing helpful feedback underscores the value of feedback, and praising people for giving effective feedback makes it more likely to be given again.

The more consistently you give and get feedback, the more normal it is. Make sure you give it right away when you begin practicing. If you wait until something negative requires feedback, then feedback will automatically be linked to the idea of a mistake. To make feedback normal, give it consistently, *especially* when participants are successful. Further, ask people to play both the giving and getting roles whenever possible, as this vests them in the process and reminds them that the person receiving feedback now will be giving it later—the roles are linked.

Make It an Everyday Thing

- The more consistently you give and get feedback, the more normal it is.
- Start giving feedback right away when you begin practicing. If you wait until something negative requires it, feedback will be linked to the idea of a mistake.
- Use sentence starters to help *everyone* give both positive and constructive feedback.

RULE 29
DESCRIBE THE SOLUTION
(NOT THE PROBLEM)

Good feedback describes the solution—in concrete, actionable terms—rather than the problem. If you were coaching a manager through his interactions with his staff, you could say, "Stop being so abrasive," but it won't provide much help in identifying alternatives. We do this all the time with children. Consider how much more effective it would be to replace a statement that describes the problem, such as "Stop fooling around!" with a statement that tells a student what to do: "Sit down at the table and start your homework."

We previously described the course our colleague Rob took while learning to ride a motorcycle. When he announced he was taking the course, we dismissed it. We assumed it was like the driver's education we had known: a mind-numbing experience in banality set in a warren of fluorescently lit rooms. But things turned out otherwise, to the degree that Rob wrote several e-mails about it so that we could apply the lessons to our own workshops:

> It's been a while since I've been in a training situation and I was blown away by how helpful that process was. There were a couple of times when I knew I didn't execute the activity properly, but I had no idea what I did wrong. That immediate and specific feedback made all the difference. Just something simple like, "Keep your head up as you're going through the turn," led to a perfect execution the next time around.

Rob described how difficult the task of driving around a simple pylon had been at first. The coach had told him that the key was his eyes. He must glance at the pylon as he approached it but keep his eyes fixed on the point he was riding toward. Apparently, if you look directly down at the pylon, that's where your body will steer the bike. But the coaches didn't discuss with Rob why this was the case until after he'd applied the feedback successfully. In the moment, they merely told him what to do. Let's reiterate that statement: they merely told him what to do. Glance down at the pylon as you approach it, but fix on the spot you are riding towards.

Now think of your own experiences in training or sports or school. How many times did someone who was tasked with coaching or teaching you fail to tell you what to do? Typically, that person might tell you what *not* to do: "Don't overhit." "Don't get caught out of position." "Don't say tactless things in meetings." Describing the solution would mean replacing "Don't overhit" with "Take a steady, even swing" or "Try to imagine you're dropping the club face onto the ball." It would replace "Don't get caught out of position" with "Stay goal-side of your man." It would replace "Don't say tactless things in meetings" with "When someone tells you what country they are from, just say you are honored or happy to meet them."

More than just telling participants what to do, describing the solution often means getting past "vague constructiveness," which is the kind of feedback that appears to tell a participant what to do but is too vague or general to be useful. Here's a quick table to compare poor feedback (which describes the problem or is only vaguely constructive) to feedback that, happily, describes the solution:

Describes the Problem	Vaguely Constructive	Describes the Solution
Don't get caught out of position.	Get in position.	Make sure you're between your man and the goal.
Don't overhit.	Take it easy.	Keep your swing steady and even.
Don't say tactless things in meetings.	Say something different next time.	Say you are honored or happy to meet them.

During scrimmage or in other settings where interruption time is limited, successful feedback has to be short. In the middle of running through high-speed presurgical procedures with your emergency room team or a dress rehearsal for *La Traviata*, there's no time to offer lengthier statements like "Adjust your lamp so it shines directly into the incision" or "Stand to the left of the dancers!" However, if you had previously offered longer descriptions of solutions during earlier stages of coaching, you can develop stock phrases, shorthand reminders of those longer pieces of feedback. You can then call them out during performance, as in the following examples:

Longer Description	Shorthand
Take a steady, even swing; imagine you're dropping the club face onto the ball.	Drop the face.
Stay goal-side of your man, and give progressively more space the farther away the ball is.	Goal-side. Space.
When someone tells you what country they are from, simply say you are honored or happy to meet them.	Honored.

Describe the Solution (Not the Problem)
- Try to move from "don't" statements that tell participants what not to do to "what to do" statements that tell them how to succeed.
- Make sure your guidance is specific and actionable.
- Look for ways to abbreviate commonly given guidance to make it easier and faster to use.

RULE 30
LOCK IT IN

Katie recently had a revealing interaction while interviewing a candidate for a job at her school. The candidate, a young teacher who we'll call Jillian with a year or two of experience under her belt, was scheduled to teach a sample lesson. Several days before, Jillian submitted her lesson plan to Katie. It was well-intentioned but disorganized and muddled: complex when straightforward would have done nicely; missing some key steps and squandering time on trivial points; sprinkled with earnest references to educational theorists. None of this was a huge surprise. We assume that we will develop smart, motivated people on the job, and we try to engineer our hiring process to reveal how an individual will respond to and use feedback.

Katie talked Jillian through the ways she should consider revising her lesson to make it stronger. They spent perhaps 20 minutes on the phone together. A day later, Jillian resubmitted her lesson plan with a pleasant note to Katie observing that she had "made all of the changes you suggested." In fact almost nothing was different. Her words said yes but her actions said no. Katie recalls having the feeling she used to get when she was a high school teacher and had given a student detailed feedback on an essay, only to receive a "revision" in which the student did little more than recopy the essay, in neater handwriting. The student would often say, "I took all of your suggestions." As it turns out, people do the darndest things—sometimes a lot more alarming than inaction—under the banner of "using your feedback." So how do you make sure they have heard what you said? The three techniques that follow can help you confirm that recipients have understood what you told them and interpreted it plausibly. They allow you to "lock it in."

Lock It In Tool 1: Summarize Feedback

One of the simplest ways to lock in feedback after you've given it is to ask the person to summarize it back to you. This gives you immediate data on whether that person heard something similar to what you thought you said. This can be especially critical when feedback is more complex and when it involves both positives and negatives. Here is a common point of confusion: you praise someone's strength and observe that it carries a downside that could be a weakness—and what they remember is the praise.

Consider a manager, Justine, who is aware that members of her team respect but don't like working with one team member, to the point that it has affected morale and results. We'll call the team member in question Carla. Justine appreciates Carla's bottom-line focus and her desire to deliver; she just wants Carla to understand that her intensity can make her come off as judgmental and pushy, and that, in turn, makes people not want to work with her. A few smiles and chortles along the way and a bit of active listening would unlock a lot of value, helping her to be productive, appreciated, and more effective in the end. So Justine has set up a meeting to work on their monthly budget together while she coaches Carla as an opportunity to practice showing her human side. Trying to keep it positive, Justine says, "One of the things I love about your work is how much intensity you bring to the team. I truly value that. I just want to make sure we get the most of it by also helping people to see the human side of you—the warmth that your kids see, for example. So let's work on our budget, but I also want you to pretend that I'm a peer. Try to practice showing warmth while we work and that you're listening to me. Try to make it explicit when you value my input."

Let's be honest for a second about Justine's feedback: like most feedback—certainly like ours much of the time—it's imperfect. She wasn't as direct as she might have been. It's just as likely that what Carla heard was that there was a problem with her colleagues—"they weren't seeing Carla's human side." Let's assume that's what happens, and that as they start working on the budget, with Carla allegedly "practicing" demonstrating warmth, it's not really coming off. There's a forced smile or two, but really, for Carla, it's all about the budget meeting. So Justine stops the meeting.

"Carla, I know we're working on the budget, and I appreciate how much progress we're making. But I know you can knock a budget meeting out with your eyes closed. Can I ask you to roll back the conversation we had at the beginning? How would you sum- marize our goals for the meeting?" What Justine is working on here is a "Roll Back"; she's asking the recipient of the feedback to tell her what she heard. It's a simple tool to check for understanding: "Tell me what I told you." The benefit is that it allows Justine to deter- mine whether Carla understood what she had asked her to do but wasn't able (or willing!) to do, or whether Carla in fact didn't understand Justine's feedback. Either way, the Roll Back can help: if the problem is with Carla's ability or willingness, having stated outright to her manager that she knows it's a priority will make her more accountable; and if the problem is that Carla didn't under- stand the feedback, Justine can try again and won't waste further time practicing without a clear purpose. She also may benefit from hearing how her feedback came across.

To some people, asking them to tell you what you told them earlier can sound patronizing. You might use it with people who are junior to you, but what if you are practicing something as a team? In that case a question can be gentler and even mutual in focus: "Should we both check our understanding here?"

Lock It In Tool 2: Prioritize Feedback

Another tool Justine could have used was to ask Carla to prioritize the feedback she'd gotten:

"Carla, I want you to focus on getting this work done in a way that is as warm and approachable as possible and that shows that you value and appreciate working together. I'm telling you that because I think your teammates don't always see that. We brainstormed some ideas for how to do that when we began this meeting. Can you take a minute to reflect on the two most important things you want to try to do during our meeting to humanize it?"

Conveniently, using this step would have many of the benefits of a Roll Back: Carla's prioritization would tell Justine a lot about whether she got the intended message, but it goes a step further and asks Carla to identify action steps that are specific. It vests Carla in the project; she's choosing the ideas that seem most actionable to her. And it holds Carla accountable for specific observable things.

Lock It In Tool 3: Next Action

Finally, Justine could have asked Carla for something even more concrete: What is she going to do first? "OK, Carla. Just to review what I know you know, you're also working here on the human side of the meeting. I want you to try to do one thing in the first two minutes to make our work together more productive from a team-building perspective. Just to make sure I see it, I want you to call your shot here. Tell me the next thing you're going to try to do."

The benefit of this approach is that it's immediate. It focuses Carla on implementing the feedback quickly and, since she's "called her shot," makes the follow-up conversation easy if it doesn't happen. "OK, we're three minutes in. Seems like this is turning out to be trickier than you expected. Let's reflect on it a bit." Or, "Good, that came off really well. Let's keep going and you tell me something else you're going to try to do."

Lock It In

- Don't assume that because you gave feedback, people interpreted it as you intended. Confirm their understanding in at
least three ways:

> Ask recipients to summarize what they heard you say.
>
> Ask recipients to prioritize the most important parts of the
> feedback you gave.
>
> Ask recipients to identify the next action they'll take to
> implement the feedback.

LEARNINGS: EXIT TICKETS

Exit tickets are a tool that great teachers use to check for understanding
at the end of their lessons. Teachers who use exit tickets devise a very
short, two-to-four-question mini-quiz before students leave their lesson
to make sure they have mastered the material. Exit tickets make
checking for understanding a regular part of every instructional session.
You can find a deeper discussion of it in Doug's book *Teach Like a
Champion*. Teachers find it helpful in making sure that students don't
leave the class knowing less than their teachers think.

Anyone giving feedback can replicate this method with a few simple
questions. Often, if/then questions are especially useful. "OK, really
quickly, let's run through a few scenarios: if *X* happened, what would
you do?" Doug once used this approach to check for understanding
of feedback he'd given his son about how to position himself on the
soccer field. They had been discussing the benefits of playing wide: on
goal kicks, Doug told his son he should move all the way to the sideline
when his goalie was kicking. As it happened, the feedback didn't work
as planned. Doug's son heard the feedback to get wide on goal kicks
and applied it to *all* goal kicks, including those when he was on the side
of the field opposite to the one where the goal kick was being taken.
He had listened too well to imprecise feedback. The next day, Doug
tried to fix his feedback. He explained the difference between strong
side and weak side and that his son should try to get as wide as he

(Continued)

could to receive the ball on the strong side (the side with the ball) and cheat to the middle just a bit when he was on the weak side (the side away from where the ball was at any time). His son quickly grasped the concept, but Doug was sensitive to the fact that his previous advice had done his son a disservice, so to check for understanding, he asked three or four quick if/then questions. "If it's a goal kick on your side, where would you go? If it was on the other side? If you were halfback and the defender on your side had the ball, where would you want to go to get open?" His son now proved he understood the feedback and was ready to apply it successfully.

CULTURE OF PRACTICE

Practice doesn't happen in a vacuum. How well practice is supported within any group or organization—be it a basketball team, a school, or a multinational corporation—can determine whether people embrace it and eagerly take on new challenges or whether they resent practice and fail to engage in it. Great practice, then, is not merely a triumph of design and engineering, but a triumph of culture. By "culture" we mean the expectations for interactions between people in the organization, as well as their core beliefs: the ideas individuals take for granted and think of as "normal" within a particular organization or system. How people think about and talk about practice in the car ride home and the days after; their ideas for their own development and improvement; and how they react to and support their peers when they are watching them practice: all are critical to the life of a talent-driven organization.

Dr. Yoon Kang, director of the Margaret and Ian Smith Clinical Skills Center at the Weill Cornell Medical College, has established a culture rooted in the practice of intentional, repetitive, and iterative activities that help turn medical students into accomplished doctors. This should come as no surprise. Medical schools are designed to be places where students learn the *practice* of medicine. But not all medical schools are created equal when it comes to creating a culture of practice. In many schools there is a culture of sink or swim. Historically, at Cornell as in most medical schools, doctors were trained to conduct intakes and physical exams in the classroom setting. Students were then sent into a hospital to conduct patient interviews, learning on the job.

With a more recent emphasis on patient safety (in 2004 the licensure to become a doctor made it a requirement for students to interact with an actor-patient), all medical schools started integrating simulated practice and role plays into their programs. "Standardized patient encounters," first used in 1963 at the University of Southern California by Dr. Howard Barrows, became the norm in medical schools across the country. Students perform exams on actor-patients who are specifically trained to follow the details of the case, making the experience as realistic as possible. This prepares students to establish rapport with patients, effectively perform examinations and other clinical skills—all necessary career benchmarks. Standardized patient encounters provide students, as early as their first year at Weill Cornell, the opportunity to perform core job tasks and get immediate feedback, a vital practice experience that could not be created with real patients this early in a doctor's career.

While all medical schools revved up their programs as a result of the changes in the licensing exam, Dr. Kang had long been dedicated to finding ways for students to better learn through practice. In particular, she thought it was critical for doctors to practice establishing rapport with patients to ensure better diagnosis and more effective treatment. At Cornell students applied this skill in the setting of the performance, diagnosing an actor-patient, responding with empathy and sensitivity, and using active listening to respond to the medical details of the case. Several studies have shown that when there is strong rapport patients are more likely to follow a doctor's advice.[1] If medical students practice only discrete clinical skills and leave med school without the ability to establish rapport, they will be less effective overall in treating their patients.

Cornell uses a lens of practice and feedback for all aspects of the program, even the design and construction of their training facility (Rule 12). Not only do they replicate the performance environment for practice; they use physical space to create a culture of practice and constant improvement. For example, a central observation area is outfitted so that faculty can observe students practicing with the actor-patients; there are one-way mirrors and the technology to support wireless headsets so that instructors can change the audio channels to observe several rooms simultaneously. Rooms are also outfitted with AV equipment and microphones so that every interaction is recorded. This creates a longitudinal database so that students and professors can track their progress and ensure that practice has a positive outcome on student performance in medical school and beyond. As we saw with the football coaches in the Introduction, coaches have long analyzed game tape, but taping practice is actually more important. Part of building a culture of practice is videotaping practice; it sends the message that improvement through practice matters.

How does your space build a culture of practice and send the message that practice is one of the most important things you do? In his article for *Harvard Magazine*, "The Twilight of the Lecture," Craig Lambert describes how Harvard physics professor Eric Mazur realized that his students were not actually learning or retaining information from his lectures. He reflects: "The students did well on textbook-style problems . . . they *floundered* on simple word problems, which demanded a real understanding of the concepts behind the formulas."[2] When he shifted his approach to focus more on active student learning and less on lecture by asking his students to discuss and explain problems to each other, students were better able to understand and retain information two months after taking his course. However, simply incorporating more active learning into all classrooms is no easy fix, and this is where the skills center at Cornell comes in. Lambert and Mazur point out that in most classrooms there is an "architectural resistance," as "most classrooms—more like 99.9 percent—on campus are auditoriums. They are built with just one purpose: focusing the attention of many on the professor."

At Cornell, where the entire space is set up for practice, observation, and feedback, a culture of practice flourishes. For the first round of feedback on practice, after a simulation, the patient takes off his actor hat and, using a detailed checklist, gives the medical student three pieces of feedback from the patient's perspective to evaluate the exchange (for example, the student did or didn't greet me by name; did or didn't listen to my heart or lungs). Actor-patients are trained to use constructive language, to tell the student how it felt to talk to the doctor, and to address the nonverbal messages the doctor was sending during the encounter. Dr. Kang says that some of the more advanced actor-patients have actually modeled the feedback for students (fulfilling the rules we described in the chapter on modeling). Following the feedback from actor-patients, students debrief with faculty, during which the emphasis is on the clinical aspects of the diagnosis. Finally, students review the video of their performance and conduct a self-assessment on their performance (Rule 22).

As we saw in Rule 23, practicing together and exchanging feedback builds isolated individuals into a collaborative team. In contrast to the cutthroat med school cultures of yore, imagine a culture based on collaborative practice and the exchange of feedback in the spirit of becoming the best doctor you can be. At Weill Cornell, aspects of everyday culture are engineered to promote effective practice and feedback. How do you create a similar environment on your team or in your organization? The rules that follow will help you on that path.

RULE 31
NORMALIZE ERROR

When you punish your people for making a mistake or falling short of a goal, you create an environment of extreme caution, even fearfulness. In sports it's similar to playing "not to lose"—a formula that often brings on defeat.

– JOHN WOODEN

We know a woman who is a breathtaking skier. She tells an interesting story about her breakthrough moment —and it was just that, a moment—when she started down the road of becoming an expert. It happened on the day she decided to fall. She was getting on the lift at the base of a steep, sunlit ski bowl. She had just come down a twisted, mogul-ridden trail in top form, earning the admiration of a teenager who'd been trailing behind her. At the bottom, amidst words like "stoked" and "killer," the teenager asked, "Do you *ever* fall?" Getting on the lift, she realized that (1) the answer was no, and that (2) if the teenager had been a nephew or a cousin whom she felt invested in developing as a skier, she wouldn't have wanted to admit that to him. Instead she would have pointed out that if you never fall, you aren't pushing yourself and you aren't improving as fast as you could be. Midway up the mountain she realized that she hardly ever fell, perhaps once every eight or ten days on skis, and even then it was usually at tangled moments when she wasn't actually skiing that hard. She realized that if she wasn't falling she probably wasn't pushing herself to learn as hard as she could be. She had gotten lazy because she was so good.

When she got to the top of the mountain and skied off the chairlift, she knew what she needed to do. She set out to ski hard enough to fall, but she was intentional about *how*. She knew that there was one thing that she had been working on: pointing her shoulders face down the mountain, no matter how steep. She then set out to execute this skill even if that meant falling. She fell three times that first day. "I could feel myself trying to do exactly the things I was afraid of. I knew if I stuck with it I would conquer my fears." She began skiing without fearing falling. Within a few weeks she was a different skier entirely.

In that single moment, she was able to embrace two important truths: first, failure is normal and not the indicator of a lack of skill; second, skiing right at the edge of mastery would make her better. She had to trust that exposing her weaknesses—risking ridicule and embarrassment—rather than trying to cover them up would be the driver of excellence. Compare our friend to a skier who just tries to ski the hardest runs as fast as he can. If he pushes himself to fall without encoding success, then he will fail miserably, likely leaning back too much on his skis and risking injury.

How do you build an organizational culture of fearless skiers willing to take thoughtful risks in order to improve—especially when the goal is to encode success? An organization has to help its people realize that failure rate and level of skill are independent variables; it has to help them feel comfortable exposing their weaknesses to their peers so they can help them improve; it has to make them feel trust and faith and even joy, not only to practice but to do so with others. The first step on that journey is to normalize error.

What does research tell us about error? *Moonwalking with Einstein* author Joshua Foer (Rule 23) found out. When Foer set out on a yearlong journey to improve his memory, he called on the "world's leading expert on expertise,"[3] Anders Ericsson, and "struck a deal." Foer gave Ericsson all of the records on his training for the United States Memory Championship. In exchange, Ericsson and his graduate students would share the data back with Foer in order to find ways to continue to improve his performance. This deal was extremely useful when Foer hit a plateau in his memory performance. Several months into his work of intense practice, his memory ceased getting better. Ericsson encouraged Foer to learn from other experts who, while engaging in "very directed, highly-focused" routines of deliberate practice, reach a performance plateau—which Foer calls the "OK Plateau." The key is to then practice failing.

To illustrate the OK Plateau, Foer discusses learning how to type. When first learning, we initially improve and improve until we ultimately reach a peak of accuracy and speed. Even though many of us spend countless hours typing in our professional and personal lives, however, we don't continue to improve. Researchers discovered that when subjects were challenged to their limits by trying to type 10–20 percent faster and were allowed to make mistakes, their speed improved. They made mistakes, fixed them, then encountered success. If Foer wanted to overcome his own performance plateau, he had to practice failing.

Applying this lesson to organizations is often easier said than done. Most organizations have a difficult relationship with error, and with good reason. Sometimes the results of error can be devastating, causing everything from a lost client, to debilitating press coverage, to massive product recalls. Even when the results would be minimal, it is common for many people in the workplace to be scared of making mistakes and even more terrified of anyone finding out. The challenge for organizations is to find appropriate ways to normalize error in the context of learning and practicing.

Here is what normalizing error looks like: first, challenge people and allow them to make mistakes, as we saw with the skier and the typist; second, respond to errors in a way that supports growth and improvement. You do this not by minimizing or ignoring mistakes, but by supporting people in fixing errors before they become too ingrained (Rule 8). This is a delicate balance, and for each organization and learning challenge it will look a bit different. To see how this balance can be achieved, let's consider the classroom, a place where learning is front and center.

Something we have learned from watching great teachers is that they are very good at creating a classroom culture where error is accepted as a normal part of learning; but these teachers don't allow errors to go uncorrected. Great teachers do not downplay the importance of an error, as in "That's OK, sweetheart, that was a hard problem. It's OK you got it wrong," and do not allow mistakes to go unaddressed. When a third-grader reads a passage aloud with a few errors, her teacher will ask her to reread the sentence or phrase that was troubling: "Try reading that sentence again." If the mistake persists, the teacher may prompt her with a decoding rule like "That sound is a short *i*." Champion teachers will be relentless in ensuring that errors don't go unaddressed and become more inscribed. They correct warmly and firmly. They prefer the rigor that self-corrections provide (as by having a student reread a challenging passage and fix her own mistake) but are direct when necessary ("That word is pronounced 'diagram'").

As in any culture, workplace, classroom, or other group, it is the accumulation of exchanges about mistakes that will determine how everyone approaches error. When a student is encouraged both to fail and to try again, it has a profound effect on all students—how they view their work individually and how they support each other in their learning efforts. The classroom becomes a safe place to fail and a place where error is always corrected but not condemned; a place where success matters.

In this effort, it's important that teachers, coaches, and managers "get past nice." Often our initial impulse when addressing error is to come at it apologetically: "That's OK, Sarah. That was a really hard one; you did your best." Or, "I'm sorry to call you out on this." This approach has a number of negative effects. It communicates lower expectations, that errors (and feedback!) are something you should apologize for, and finally that error is something to be avoided. When you do too much tap dancing around something that needs to be improved, people will think that it is a bigger deal than it really is. Be warm, be direct, get past nice, and make errors a normal part of practice.

SAY IT THIS WAY

How you frame error is critical. Finding the right language and hitting the right tone can have an amazing normalizing effect. Consider, for example, the following sentence starters:

- "I'm so glad you did that; it's one of the most common mistakes that we make when trying X."
- "You did that for all of the right reasons; what you need to look out for is X."

Or bring in your own personal experience in learning a particular skill:

- "You just did what I did when I first learned X."

How error is addressed can make a huge difference in a group's culture. As people pick up on the language and the attitude it conveys, their approach to their own mistakes and the mistakes of others will change. Mistakes may increase but so will everyone's expectations of themselves and each other.

Failing, too, responds to practice. We practice failure in our schools with our students. At the beginning of the year, we practice what happens when students make errors in judgment and get a consequence for misbehavior. We explicitly tell them how to respond; we model how students should respond to a consequence (for example, by keeping their head up and focusing on fixing their behavior); and then we have students practice how they will respond when they get a consequence. What does practicing failure look like in other settings? If you work in customer service, you could practice having a phone call with a customer in which the customer service representative has tried everything but the issue can't be resolved. The only thing for the rep to do is practice apologizing and responding immediately when the customer asks to speak to a supervisor. What is the rule that we always learned when falling off a bike or a horse? Get back on. Practice how to respond to failure.

In this book we began our discussion on practice with the importance of encoding success. What is the relationship between the need to practice success and the need to normalize error? What you do in practice is practice succeeding. But when practice is well designed, you can also use it to isolate failure. This allows people to take calculated risks in order to improve at a particular skill. When failure happens in your organization, you want to have built a culture that embraces it. When you effectively normalize error, what starts with failure reliably ends in success. The process of encoding success is what makes failure safe.

Normalize Error

- Encourage people to challenge themselves and push beyond their performance plateaus by taking calculated risks in practice.
- Don't minimize or ignore errors, or they will become too ingrained and people won't learn from them.
- Help performers identify their own errors so that they can improve them independently.
- Practice responding to errors in an effort to prepare for and normalize mistakes.

RULE 32
BREAK DOWN THE BARRIERS TO PRACTICE

What looks like resistance is often a lack of clarity.
– DAN AND CHIP HEATH, *SWITCH*

Practice, especially when done in front of others, can be physiologically challenging. For many of us it can actually bring on negative physical reactions (racing heart, sweaty palms) and psychological reactions (fear, nervousness, angst). But a fear of failing in front of our colleagues can prevent a level of success that can only be realized through practicing in front of others. While practicing privately is important, unless you also practice in front of others you miss out on the valuable feedback necessary to making improvements. As musical great Itzhak Perlman told Atul Gawande in a 2012 article for the *New Yorker*, practicing in front of others gives you an "extra ear."[4] We mustn't be afraid of the critical lens brought by extra pairs of eyes and ears as we work to improve.

Because people would rather work on what's easy to work on than on what is psychologically difficult, you need to be prepared for the clever ways that people will find to "work around the work." These are the *barriers to entry* you'll need to help people overcome if they are to engage in the kind of practice that can build a culture of learning and improvement. These barriers may come in the form of embarrassment, fear of failure, or lack of trust in the process. After the initial resistance is overcome, adults can then engage deeply in practice, but some force has to propel them over that initial barrier. In our own work, when we started to infuse practice into our workshops for teachers and school leaders, we found that the time to begin practice coincided with the sudden need for participants to take bathroom breaks. If participants weren't sprinting off to the bathroom, then they were averting their eyes or urgently searching for something in their bags. While not entirely surprising, these escape tactics are a large part of the barriers to entry. Here are a few ways participants have used barriers to avoid practice:

- *"Hey, we're working hard here."* Putting on a display of hard work and active engagement can be a tactic for avoiding practice (Rule 24). In a recent workshop, during what was supposed to be a role play in which teachers work on their nonverbal directions to students, we noticed a group engaged in active debate on the topic. Upon noticing a facilitator nearby, one of the group members piped up, "We got into a really deep discussion of this." Most people would think that's good: they were on task, deeply engaged in the content. At first we did too, and we left them alone to reflect. But then we realized that these participants were on topic, not on task. They were (creatively) avoiding practice.

- *"I don't believe in . . ."* One of our practice activities asks teachers to teach students the Pledge of Allegiance so that they can practice giving nonverbal redirections to students who are off task (Rule 10). We intentionally use the pledge because most people can recite it without having to think, thus freeing up their brains for practicing the skill we want to work on. One skeptical teacher took this opportunity to say that he didn't want to teach the Pledge of Allegiance because he didn't believe in it. We saw immediately that he was objecting to an extraneous piece of the activity in order to avoid the actual practice. We had him teach a nursery rhyme instead, and once we pushed him over his initial barrier to practice, he successfully engaged in the practice activity. It was important that we didn't allow his discomfort with an ancillary aspect of the activity to prevent him from practicing, and we discovered our own ability to push past discomfort in the name of creating a culture of practice.

- *"This doesn't seem very realistic."* Others may resist practice by claiming that a scenario doesn't "feel very realistic," without realizing that we are intentionally distorting reality in order to be able to practice. Dr. Yoon Kang has witnessed this in her program with medical students. "Initially," she says, "the hardest thing about practice is that they [the students] know it's 'practice.' Before they walk in the room, students have challenges suspending reality. Once they walk in the room you see it melt away." In our work, we see participants resist activities because of the level of scripting that we do for them. For example, in the Lay-Up Drill, when we ask teachers to give the direction "I need you to sit up" in order to focus on nonverbal body language (like planting your feet or using a signal), participants sometimes resist by saying that they wouldn't actually use the exact words "I need you to sit up." They are tripped up by the words we ask them to use, even though the words aren't the point of the exercise.

Here are some steps leaders and coaches can take to address barriers to entry:

1. *Identify and name the barriers.* Confront head-on that which is preventing practice. Provide a name for the roadblocks your people are encountering and then practice overcoming them (yes, through practice!). Stress the importance of learning as a team and of having the humility to try.

2. *Help people get over barriers by practicing (privately if necessary).* Don't belabor the point: identify the barriers, normalize them, and then dive into the practice. One school leader we know was working with a particularly resistant teacher on improving her ability to give clear directions. When he first suggested that they practice, she begrudgingly began by stating three clear directions that she gives in her class. But it was obvious that she was not engaged, as she pushed back every chance she got. When he noted her resistance and asked her to practice giving him one direction as though he were her most challenging student, she started practicing this small skill, repeating it over and over, until she began to notice an improvement. Her demeanor started to change; she became more open to his feedback; and ultimately she improved. This school leader was able to break down a teacher's barrier to practice through the practice itself. And he did this by practicing with her one-on-one. Allowing people who are particularly resistant to practice in a one-on-one setting can help them overcome fears they may have for public practice. It is perhaps one of the most underutilized forms of practice.

3. *Then don't talk about it anymore.* Know the end goal: your people will practice. There are no legitimate reasons not to practice. If needed, play your trump card: "I hear what you are saying. Let's

suspend our disbelief, but we're going to try it and see how it goes. We'll keep those concerns in mind as we try it." The practice itself will get them to believe. Once you start, the process itself builds buy-in. As the leader, operate with a sense of faith that they will feel a sense of triumph after practice.

SAY IT THIS WAY

Bringing our fears and insecurities about practice to the surface by naming them can be the first step in preventing them from interfering with practice. For example, you might say,

- "It can be awkward to role-play, but . . ."
- "It is challenging to simulate, but . . ."
- "I know I initially had a huge fear of embarrassment, but . . ."

Always follow the "buts" with a description of the importance of practice and why a particular activity will be so incredibly valuable for preparation, improvement, and the acquisition of particular skills.
Walk people through the recipe:

- "At first this may be awkward. But I think you'll find it really helpful."
- "We're going to do this together, and at the very least, if you don't like it, we're going to be done soon."

You just want people to start. Planning what you want to say (and practicing it!) is an important first step in getting your people to engage in practice.

Some of us have learned not to believe in practice because of the pervasive ineffective use of practice. Maybe we have been embarrassed by practice that was unintentionally not set up to help us succeed, and we remain self-conscious. Or perhaps we have never had opportunities for micropractice (Rule 7) and therefore haven't effectively built the smaller skills required to master larger ones.

We are the nonbelievers because we haven't experienced effective practice. The skeptics also don't believe, but not because of negative experiences. Usually they don't believe because being skeptical has proven to be an effective defense mechanism against practice, which may expose weaknesses. Regardless of the barriers, once you effectively address them, the benefits of practice can be realized. When people don't want to volunteer or they resist practice in other ways, meet their coping mechanisms head-on by describing them and then overcoming them through practice. Only by proactively addressing these barriers to entry will you be able to create an organizational culture rooted in practice. The next rule on practicing joyfully can also help.

LEARNINGS: "LET'S TRY IT"

Jonathon, the dean of curriculum at a K–8 school in the Midwest, observed one of his fifth-grade teachers teaching a lesson on identifying vocabulary in context. He had observed how she modeled using context clues to identify the meaning of the word but noticed that she did it from a test-taking perspective, inserting possible meanings into the sentence to see if the words made sense but not asking students to use the context clues to infer meaning.

Jonathon followed up the lesson he observed with an e-mail: "I know you're going to teach a similar lesson tomorrow. Let's meet tomorrow morning before your lesson and practice the first part of your lesson to make sure your instruction on context clues is clear and sharp."

When the teacher arrived at his office, she was clearly not enthusiastic or energized about what was ahead. Jonathon knew that her low affect was not a reflection of a lack of desire to improve her instruction but about how discouraged she was feeling. But he dove right in and asked her to start practicing the first part of her lesson. When she began practicing, she was sitting down. Jonathon asked her to stand because he knew she wasn't going to teach the lesson sitting down (Rule 12).

She started to practice but again was flustered and uncomfortable. It was evident that she didn't have a clear plan for how she was going to start her lesson. She continued practicing and went through the first

(Continued)

part of the lesson; when she actually got into the modeling part of her lesson, it was pretty good. Jonathon was able to point out what was strong in her lesson (her modeling) and what needed sharpening (the introduction to new material). He told her, "This is what you might say. . . . Let's try it." They practiced it a few more times, and each time her energy perked up. Once she finally got it down, she did it again. And then, on her own, on the final round, she stood up to teach. Her introduction to her lesson was finally strong. She left with more energy and enthusiasm than she had come into the meeting with.

This teacher went into class that morning eager to go teach because she felt more prepared. She and Jonathon had dealt with her frustration and resistance to practice by just diving into the practice. This gave her the confidence and the skills to actually get better. Continuing to talk about her feelings wouldn't have translated into improved instruction (nor would it have improved her emotions). When you find people resisting practice, sometimes the best response is simply to ask them to give it a try.

Break Down the Barriers to Practice

* Anticipate that some people in your organization will resist practice.
* Identify and name the barriers to entry that you observe.
* Overcome the barriers by diving into practice.

RULE 33
MAKE IT FUN TO PRACTICE

Work without joy is drudgery. Drudgery does not produce champions, nor does it produce great organizations.

– JOHN WOODEN

Some aspects of practice are just naturally fun, but what do we do when the fun parts aren't the ones that help us get better? Many amateur golfers have had the experience of feeling like a pro at the range, hitting countless balls long and straight—only to go onto the course the next day and be disappointed to see their success on the range not translate to their scorecard. In a *New York Times* blog, Laird Small, the 2003 PGA teacher of the year, asserts that this is "because at the driving range, people hit golf balls" but "on the course, we have to hit golf shots."[5] On the range, recreational golfers may fire off a bucket of 25 balls in a half hour or so and then pack up their clubs, often feeling accomplished. When the pros go to the range, however, they simulate the speed of a real golf game by hitting half that many balls over the same amount of time. Phil Mickelson's coach Butch Harmon, who also coached Tiger Woods, points out how much the average golfer could learn from watching how a pro approaches the range. He asks, "Who plays golf by raking one ball after another into the same place while hitting the same club? Nobody, right? So why do people practice like that?"[6]

Any recreational golfer will agree, though, that it is much more fun and rewarding to launch a driver high and far in the air, with the immediate positive feedback—"ping!"—than it is to spend time chipping out of the sand or practicing an approach shot. But it's those shots that have the greatest impact on your success on the course. Mike Bender and Laird Small, both among the top-ten golf coaches in the nation, suggest a simple change in your approach. If you make practicing the short game fun, you will want to practice and your scores will go down (in golf, the desired direction). Make it a competition, either with yourself or a friend. See how many consecutive four-foot putts you can sink; who can get closer to the hole on two shots from the bunker; or how many chips it takes you to hit a nickel on the green. Make it fun to practice the skills you need to actually get better.

Practice should not be a punishment. When you invest the time and creativity to make practice fun, people will be motivated to participate, not only out of sheer enjoyment but also because you are communicating an important message: this is something positive that is worth our time.

Many tasks that we need to master in order to improve and develop are, like the short game in golf, just plain hard. But other tasks we may resist because they are tedious. The program Mavis Beacon Teaches Typing made learning to type (an incredibly tedious task when first undertaken) fun by making it into a game. Mavis Beacon Teaches consists of different speed and accuracy tests, which constantly track the typist's speed in words per minute, and several competitive games. Simply typing different sentences over and over to improve speed and accuracy would not motivate a beginning typist to practice. But if that same typist is typing to race a cartoon car against another car or competing against a fictional person typing the same sentences, then practicing becomes more fun and more motivating. The student wants to practice and therefore does it longer and more often. The typist gets better.

We have tried to apply the following ideas in our own workshops, having often seen great teachers take a similar approach to infusing joy into their classrooms:

• *Leverage the Camaraderie of Practice.* Being a part of a team is a welcome change for people who work in isolation. If you are a doctor or a teacher, for example, you gain camaraderie from working with your peers through practice. At our two-day workshops we frequently see teachers and leaders who have worked in silos all year coming together as they take risks and have fun through practice. Having the opportunity to share stories and strategies and to solve problems through practicing with your colleagues, when you normally work by yourself, can offer fresh perspectives, new ideas, and most of all, fun.

• *Find the Fun in the Objective.* Though incorporating joy is important, you should still have a clear objective and purpose to your practice (Rule 5). Incorporating fun is most effective when it is intricately connected to the objective. If a soccer coach's players love to play dodgeball, he may be tempted to have them play as part of warm-up, rationalizing that it's a way to warm up muscles before stretching. Instead, he could make the objective a particular skill (like dribbling) and create a drill which is fun but also focuses on the skill. So he might have his players all dribble their ball simultaneously as he or another player tries to kick their balls away from them; when he is able to kick a ball away, the player is eliminated. Get the most out of the practice by making joy serve the objective.

• *Make It a Competition.* Children aren't the only ones who enjoy a good competition. Turning something into a competition often requires only a small tweak in the activity. For example, during a training in which reading teachers were learning how to use a nonfiction reading strategy, we came up with a way to take what was a lackluster activity and transform it into a competition. Initially, we asked teachers to read a passage from a fiction text and underline the sections that mention topics that would serve as an opportunity to have students read a nonfiction article to get more background information. Though centered on a clear objective, it was not very fun. So we turned it into a "parlor game" in which teachers found promising passages from fiction, wrote them on small pieces of paper, and put them into a hat. Teachers then drew the passages out of the hat and tried to come up with as many ways to increase students' background knowledge for a particular passage. A simple activity became fun, and teachers better remembered the skill they were practicing. Simple prizes and rewards like small gift cards or homemade trophies are a good way to sweeten the pot.

• *Three Cheers!* Throughout our workshops, we incorporate quick cheers (that we have learned from great teachers) to give to participants following practice. They are admittedly goofy, but they can effectively lighten the mood while recognizing participants for their hard work. Following a role play in which teachers teach a mini-lesson using "Wait Time" (the time they wait after asking a question until they call on a student), we may then give participants the "roller-coaster cheer" by quickly modeling it and then having them do it (pushing your hands in the air six times to mimic a roller coaster going up a hill, and then three times going down, saying, "wooo! wooo! wooo!"). You may have to take our word for it, but it's fun.

- *Suspense and Surprise.* In order to ensure that all participants eventually get a chance to practice (instead of only those most likely to volunteer), you can randomly assign roles by hiding Post-its under their chairs ("You're the first surgeon to practice today"), or by whose birthday is coming up next or who commutes the longest to work each day. This type of framing prevents the rally-killing plea, "Any volunteers?" It is especially useful when you are training large groups and ultimately saves valuable time for the actual practice and feedback components (Rule 15). It keeps the practice fresh, fun, and engaging. It is no longer *if* someone will volunteer to practice, but *who.* The element of surprise has another key benefit. By keeping the practice role unknown in these ways, all participants approach role plays and practice as though they may be the one who will be chosen next to practice. This results in people authentically doing the work to prepare, which is practice in itself.

The more your team members enjoy doing something, the more they will practice. The more they practice, the more they will improve. In our trainings we tout that one of the results of our workshops will be happy teachers, because effective teachers are happy teachers. But when you or your team need a little added incentive to practice, keep the above ideas in mind. Remember first and foremost not to use practice as a punishment or only when performance has been poor. The power of practice, and the joy of fulfillment it can bring, will be undermined if it is only prompted by failure. People won't be invested, because they will be distracted by the implications of what it means to be asked to practice. The next rule addresses this: how to make practice the norm for yourself or your organization.

Make It Fun to Practice
- Utilize friendly and positive competition (for individuals or between individuals).
- While striving to make practice fun, always maintain the objective of the practice.
- Encourage your players to cheer for each other in practice (not just in the game).
- Incorporate elements of surprise. Keep people on their toes by asking all participants to plan and by surprising the next person to be called to practice. (It's also a useful accountability tool!)

RULE 34
EVERYBODY DOES IT

Frequently in our workshops, we encounter senior-level leaders who really like the material that we are presenting and believe in using it in their organizations. We initially were surprised when we noticed that these leaders often weren't practicing. We approached one executive director who was standing on the sidelines while the other participants engaged in a role play who said, "I don't really do this in my job." It is much easier to sit in the back of the room with a laptop, observing others taking risks, and think how powerful the practice is, without having to take those risks ourselves.

But we have also witnessed the opposite reaction from senior leaders, and the impact on others has been tremendous. One afternoon during a training with 60 teacher leaders at the Houston Independent School District (HISD), we were practicing a technique we call "No Opt Out," which has teachers hold individual students accountable for the right answer. At one point, teachers were practicing how to respond if a student refuses to answer a question by saying "I don't know" in a sarcastic tone. Anastasia Lindo Anderson, a school improvement officer for HISD Middle Schools (no small role, as she is responsible for helping principals across Houston improve their instructional programs), and her colleagues from the district were practicing along with their teachers. When asked if she would share her practice, she gladly accepted. We all watched as she and the teacher role-playing the sarcastic student went back and forth. It wasn't easy. The "student" continued to resist despite her warm persistence. What she ultimately was able to model was respectful but insistent language and a tone that served as an excellent example. Her willingness to expose herself and share her expertise not only helped teachers see a great way to leverage the technique, but showed her openness to engaging in practice. She wasn't just modeling a technique. She was modeling risk-taking, engagement, and a commitment to improving.

At our workshops we now model all of our practice activities in advance of having participants practice, and we sometimes call our shot saying that we will model a B+ version. We then intentionally make a few small errors and ask for feedback (this allows us to model the structure of our practice activities with feedback and then the incorporation of the feedback). If you are nervous about modeling as a leader, framing your modeling as a B+ version gives you permission to try it because you are being transparent with your staff that you are not going to be perfect. This serves several purposes: (1) it takes the pressure off of you if you are new to modeling; (2) it models the feedback process; and (3) it helps your team see you as someone who is willing to engage in practice. It shows that just because you're the leader doesn't mean that you're perfect. This goes a long way in building trust and a culture of practice.

When you are ready, you can take this up a level: don't frame it as a B+ version; just jump into the modeling (after you have planned it). Say, "I'm just going to try this." This framing shows the level of risk that you are willing to take for the purposes of practicing and improving. Always ask for feedback when you model. This shows that everybody practices, and that everybody gets feedback in practice. In our workshops, after modeling practice activities, we always ask, "What is something I could have done better?" This is usually met with silence. People are trying to be nice, and they are reluctant to give us feedback. But we always push them on this in the spirit of creating a culture of practice. People assume that as leaders we shouldn't be corrected. They are socialized to believe that we aren't really asking for feedback. We have to persist: "I know there were at least three things I could have improved. What's one of them?" When we set this expectation in the beginning as we establish a culture of practice, by the end of our workshops participants are more than willing to share their feedback.

SAY IT THIS WAY

Being thoughtful and intentional about your language can support a culture of practice. For example, asking, "Are there any volunteers to try this out?" can be a real culture killer. Subtly changing the request by asking, "Who's going to try first?" or "Here's a great chance to practice and get better—Who wants it?" can make the difference between no one and several people being willing to take the risk. This shift in language can overcome barriers to entry and ensure that all members of your team take a risk required in practice. Asking who wants to try first communicates that everybody is going to be getting a chance to try—it's just a question of who is going to go first.

As we saw earlier, we all may experience our own barriers to entry. When you are intentional and inviting in your language, everybody in your organization will be more willing to try. When you are intentional with your language *and* you engage in practice as the leader, you have the necessary ingredients for creating a culture where everybody practices. As we saw in the chapter on modeling, it is vital that we provide an effective model if we want practice to be effective; it's also vital if we want to build a culture of practice. If you don't personally embrace practice as the leader—and practice yourself—then a culture of practice will never thrive in your organization.

Everybody Does It

- As the leader, be willing to model and engage in practice yourself.
- Ask for feedback on your practice in order to model getting past nice.
- Use language that is inviting and assumes everybody will practice.

RULE 35
LEVERAGE PEER-TO-PEER ACCOUNTABILITY

While rebuilding houses destroyed by Hurricane Mitch in Nicaragua in 1998, a Peace Corps volunteer started a credit union requiring people receiving a new home to put down community references in lieu of collateral. These references were friends, family members, or neighbors who could vouch that the applicants would pay the loan. The decision to create these arrangements was based on microfinance—the idea that people would be more likely to default on their own possessions than to compromise their reputation in the community and let their community down—and it proved to be effective. With microfinance, the rate at which people in developing nations pay back their loans exceeds any predictive algorithm that bankers may use. One of the biggest factors that reduces the number of people defaulting is that microloans are issued to a group whose members jointly commit to repayment. According to a 2006 study on microfinance by Suresh Sundaresan, professor of finance and economics at Columbia University, and PhD candidate Sam Cheung, joint liability helps "keep the default rates of members low" and "active peer monitoring reduces defaults and delinquencies." It also "prevents any member of the group from taking on risky projects because others in the group, who are jointly liable will attempt to prevent that from happening."[7] When individuals owe people close to them instead of an anonymous big bank, they are more motivated by their loyalties and relationships than they are by having their credit threatened.

How can we apply these principles in creating a culture of practice? Consider the idea that people are at least as accountable to their peers as they are to authority. Leveraging that commitment in training can be a valuable tool in promoting an effective culture of practice. A powerful way to create a culture of peer accountability (and therefore practice) is through the self-identification of areas of growth and mutual accountability.

At one of our best schools, North Star Academy's Vailsburg Elementary, principal Julie Jackson focuses on three things: systems and routines, positive framing, and strong voice. She trains in these areas over and over, choosing to practice fewer things better and never wavering from those top three (following Rule 2). She also recognizes the power in having her team exercise a degree of choice in what they work on and how. She asks her teachers to identify the techniques they want to improve. This gives them constrained choices for the areas of improvement, but it also gives them the freedom to decide what they are going to focus on, both individually and as a team. Teachers are more invested in the practice of each technique because they identify their areas of growth themselves. They then work together in small teams, making commitments to each other about how they are going to practice and achieve their goals. As a result, they hold each other accountable by practicing the techniques together and then observing each other in the classroom for the specific techniques. Ask your team to set goals and to hold each other accountable, and you will reap the benefits of a culture of practice.

At many of our schools we often start the year with a brief discussion on a concept we learned from Ronald Morrish's *With All Due Respect*. In the book, Morrish introduces the idea that at successful schools—schools where teachers, students, and families are working together towards a common goal—teachers see themselves as "school teachers," not "classroom teachers." That means that teachers are invested in each other's success and that all teachers are responsible for the teaching and learning of all children in their school, not just those students in their classroom. When they see another teacher in trouble, school teachers seek to help them instead of judge or ridicule them. The sad reality today is that many of our schools are full of classroom teachers, teachers who walk by unsuccessful classrooms and roll their eyes, thinking, "Those students behave with me." Classroom teachers subscribe to a "shut my door and teach" mentality. They believe that they have one responsibility: to teach *their* kids. This type of culture is poisonous. It's poisonous to the development of teachers, and it's poisonous to children. According to Morrish, "For discipline to work in a school, you must adopt the following belief: 'Together, we are the teachers of all the students at our school.' . . . Unless each teacher ascribes to this bigger picture, school-wide discipline cannot be implemented."[8] In a culture of practice where people are invested in each other's success and development, teachers improve and students learn, schools are better, and so is our society.

No matter what sector you work in, you can apply the "school teacher" mentality. Invite your team to work together to identify and set their own goals. Allow them to determine what they should be practicing, and make them accountable to each other. When individuals are invested in each other's success, your team will be inherently stronger. Members of your team will support each other in practicing to achieve their goals, and a culture of practice will flourish. When your team members are invested in each other, their successes become inextricably linked and getting better as a team becomes much more achievable.

Leverage Peer-to-Peer Accountability

- Allow your team to self-identify particular skills and areas of growth they want to focus on (based on consistent feedback).
- Encourage team members to make mutual commitments to each other.

RULE 36
HIRE FOR PRACTICE

In our work in schools, we learned very early in our process that we needed to see people teach a sample lesson before we hired them to teach in our schools. It may sound absurd that this was a revelation, but the majority of schools in our country don't ask prospective teachers to actually teach a lesson before hiring them. On his "School Reform" blog, Whitney Tilson cites that only 13 percent of teachers hired in the Los Angeles Unified School District in 2010 were required to teach a sample lesson before they were hired.[9] This is the equivalent of hiring 100 surgeons when you had seen only 13 of them perform surgery. We soon realized though that it wasn't just about candidates demonstrating that they could teach a sample lesson in our schools. What we became most interested in was their ability to respond to feedback—how candidates take it and how they are able to incorporate it into their instruction. In the feedback session, we often ask candidates to repeat a particular part of the lesson, practicing with school leaders. What teachers do in the sample lesson is important, but it's more important to see how they do in the feedback session.

Katie and another teacher leader at her school recently conducted a feedback session with a teacher candidate after her sample lesson. To practice, Katie used the teacher leader to act as the student with her head down on the desk and had the candidate ask her to sit up straight. Katie had her do it three or four times, each time asking her to incorporate a different piece of feedback. The candidate remained positive and open to feedback throughout the process, which gave Katie a good understanding of how she might perform within her culture of practice.

Whatever the practice task is for your candidates, focus mostly on how they respond to the feedback process. Are they resilient or resistant to the process? Do they see it as an unwelcome challenge, or are they excited about the level of feedback they are getting? This process not only informs hiring decisions but also better serves your potential hires. If candidates don't enjoy the process, then they likely won't enjoy working in an environment in which practice and improvement are the focus.

The more we have come to understand that we have to grow our teachers and that the way to grow them is through practice, the more we focus on how we use practice in our selection process. It has caused us to realize that we don't always need to hire the very best teacher but a teacher who is most susceptible to practice. We would rather have a level-six teacher (on a scale of ten) who has the potential to skyrocket than a level-eight teacher who will have a slower learning curve and potentially be resistant to practice and feedback. Though we hire for being coachable, we can also coach people to be more coachable, so we look for that too.

Assume that you are hiring people who will stay with your organization for at least five years. In that case, it's more important to think about where they will be in their second year, after one year of practicing and coaching, versus where they enter in year one. If you have someone practice and he is a six out of ten, but is open to practice and feedback, then he could be a valuable contribution to your culture of practice. On his way to becoming a level eight, he may make other eights into nines through his relentless spirit of improvement. You may be better served to hire an employee with a lot of potential through practice than someone who is fantastic but could potentially be a drain on a culture of relentless improvement.

Building an organization around practice means hiring people who are responsive to it: people who like and use feedback, who enjoy working with a team, who are comfortable talking about their mistakes, and who are eager to improve. In short, incorporating practice into your hiring changes your selection process because it changes the attributes you are looking for.

Set candidates up to have an informal interaction with someone who would be their subordinate. Are they respectful and polite or dismissive? Are they receptive to feedback from colleagues, regardless of their positional authority? For a candidate applying for a position in advertising, ask her to create a mini-campaign for a new product line. Is it innovative? When you give her feedback on her innovation, is she excited to incorporate it? For a candidate in corporate real estate, ask him to prepare a pitch for one of the buildings you are trying to sell. Does he have a sense of the market? Is he aware of what clients want? How does he respond to a simulated situation in which a client doesn't like what he has prepared? Is he receptive to feedback? You probably see a theme here. Though candidates' performance on these tasks is important, it is of equal importance to see how they respond to the experience of practicing and getting feedback. As part of the interview process, ask candidates to try out different approaches based on feedback, and see if they can improve through practice, or if they are resistant to it.

When Erica first interviewed to work at an Uncommon school as a dean, she prepared intensively for her "sample lesson." Despite hours of preparation and practice, Erica's lesson was a disaster. Several students were talking when she was talking; a student who was distracting others on the carpet had to be sent to his desk; and she didn't effectively transition students from their desks back to the carpet for the lesson wrap-up. Yet she still got the job. Why? Because they were hiring not only for Erica's skills in the classroom but also for her ability to take honest feedback, reflect on her own instruction, and identify action steps she could have taken to improve her lesson. In the lesson debrief, Erica identified about 15 ways she would have taught the lesson differently. ("I should have observed in the classroom beforehand to understand more of the classroom's routines and procedures." "I should have circulated more when students were on the carpet.") She was eager for input and feedback from her interviewers. Afterwards, thinking that she had completely bombed the interview, she called her husband and told him that it had been a good experience but there was no way she was getting the position. Little did she know at the time that her reaction to feedback and her willingness to try again would actually get her the job.

When school leaders give feedback to potential candidates, they often say, "If you were my teacher, this is what I would say to you about your lesson. . . ." You can immediately tell how willing candidates are to practice and respond to constructive criticism by how they react to the feedback that follows. Are they writing it down? Are they nodding their head? Are they pushing back on suggestions or making excuses for their actions? These are all incredibly useful data points; more useful than an answer on their beliefs about pedagogy or theory. Ask them to practice their instruction, practice reflecting on the lesson, and then practice getting feedback on its strengths and areas for improvement. Finally, have them teach a portion of the lesson again to you, incorporating the feedback. In short, ask them to do what they would have to do on the job.

Consider the skills that are required for your profession but that are not susceptible to improvement through practice. Hire for these skills. If reasonable practice won't improve required skills (like basic people skills and social graces), then hire people who already possess them. Identify those skills that are prerequisites and interview (or do a phone screen) to determine if candidates possess them. Then, identify those skills that *can* be practiced and have candidates simulate a practice activity to determine if they can develop and improve these skills. Incorporate practice into your lens for hiring new employees and you will have a greater chance of creating a strong team rooted in a culture of practice.

Hire for Practice
- Before hiring your team, thoughtfully consider the practice task you want potential employees to demonstrate.
- When potential hires practice, use the opportunity to gauge their openness to practice and feedback.
- Ask them to repeat a portion of the practice task. Evaluate their ability to actively incorporate your feedback.

RULE 37
PRAISE THE WORK

We have discussed how to develop skills through the use of praise in single interactions, working one-on-one (Rule 26). It's important to also think about positive feedback at scale across an organization. In developing a culture of practice, organizations can support the effective use of praise in two vital ways: first, through normalizing effective praise that encourages good practice; and second, through creating strong systems of recognition. Whether it is your middle school soccer team or Six Sigma Black Belts at General Electric, people respond to praise. But it is all too easy for recognition to become a meaningless exercise. When awards are given away to everyone, when praise is distributed freely and disingenuously, or when praise focuses on traits rather than actions, it can be useless at best and at worst can be destructive.

Often-cited Stanford social psychologist Carol Dweck has studied the impact of praise on student achievement. Her work has demonstrated that when you praise children for a particular trait (for example, being smart) instead of a replicable action (for example, working diligently on a challenging set of math problems), students may actually underperform because they don't see their achievement as being within their control. Praising traits leads students to believe either "I'm smart" or "I'm not," whereas praising actions leads them to believe they can change their behavior to influence outcomes. We should learn from Dweck's work when working with both children and adults in practice. Praise the actions that you want to see from your players, your children, or your employees, and these actions will multiply.

Watching stellar teachers use precise praise to motivate and inspire students has taught us a lot about how we can do the same with adults. We've learned that it's important to differentiate acknowledgment from praise, setting a higher standard for when praise is used. As Doug describes in *Teach Like a Champion*, "In a case where expectations have been met an acknowledgement is fitting, a simple description of what the student did or even a thank-you usually suffices."[10] Acknowledging your students, your children, your players, or your employees is important. "Thanks for helping out your teammate." "Thanks for clearing the dishes." "Thanks for your comments in today's meeting." These statements recognize when expectations have been *met*. You *expect* your players to help their teammates, your kids to clear their plates, and your employees to actively participate in meetings. Praise, however, should be reserved for when people go above and beyond the call of duty or when they truly demonstrate excellence. "That was fantastic of you to clear and clean all of our dishes tonight!" "It was great of you to collect all of the balls and jerseys after practice today." "You were outstanding in how you delivered that really difficult message today in the staff meeting. I'm proud of you for tackling such a difficult issue because it will make a difference in our performance and communication." Acknowledge (by saying "thank you") behavior that meets expectations; praise behavior that exceeds it.

Using precise praise in the classroom, we have learned the importance of giving it genuinely and earnestly. Adults and kids alike can immediately perceive when praise is not genuine. When praise is delivered insincerely, it can be cloying and can undermine what you are trying to recognize. Balance sincere praise with candor and constructive criticism, and your praise will be valued.

Use genuine praise in practice and in performance, and use it publicly. Praise is often most powerful when it is made publicly because it gives the recipient the attention that she deserves and, further, it informs others of the actions that your team or organization values. One way to bring important positive feedback to everyone's attention is through systems of recognition that support effective practice. Make sure that these systems extend not only to performance (for example, writing a weekly e-mail to your sales team in which you praise one of your employees: "Anthony knocked it out of the park in today's presentation to our client!") but to practice as well ("Jen incorporated a new strategy today when we practiced our closing arguments"). Having a system of recognition that extends to practice is especially important because the positive feedback can inform people on what to do during performance. It also ensures that you won't just praise success ("Sheila was promoted!") but that you will praise the habits that lead to success.

With one of our practice activities in which every teacher gets individual feedback from a coach, we found that teachers weren't listening to the feedback that other teachers were getting because they wanted to give each other privacy. We encouraged them to fight that instinct, because the feedback and praise that individual teachers were getting also benefited the entire group. When others could hear the praise, they could identify actions that they could strive to replicate. When people know how to make praise specific and applicable, making it publicly contributes powerfully to a culture of practice and improvement.

In creating systems of recognition, Uncommon Schools has set up a bulletin board in its central office in which employees post public praise that recognizes how their colleagues may be demonstrating the core values of the organization. A recent post made by the director of marketing celebrated the chief information officer for "making time to listen and provide feedback on a presentation my interns prepped. They felt professional and respected to have time with and be engaging with the CIO." This praise fulfilled all of the ideal tenets of using precise praise: it praised actions, not traits; it went beyond acknowledgment because the action warranted praise; it was done publicly; and it was genuine. And the two most powerful components? It was about *practice*, and it was delivered by someone other than the CEO.

Praise the Work
- Normalize praise that supports good practice:
    Praise actions, not traits
    Differentiate acknowledgment from praise
    Be genuine
- Create systems of recognition.

■ ■ ■

Creating a culture of practice is not simple work. The rules in this chapter can help you begin to master the challenges that lie ahead. One of the benefits of a robust culture—an organization that loves to improve and that thinks about mistakes as a normal part of improving—is the sense of camaraderie that develops among peers who take time to build each other up, mutually expose their weaknesses, praise one another's strengths, and demonstrate the humility implied in the decision to risk falling. Practice together, then, and make your profession a team sport. These rules will push you to intentionally plan for strong, safe practice that will help you get better at making your people better.

POST-PRACTICE

Making New Skills Stick

A marketing company we'll call NewBrands was looking to boost company morale in order to more effectively retain employees who were leaving for competing firms. In exit interviews, employees consistently cited an unsupportive work environment as a main cause for their departure. The company was worried about the increasing cost of training new hires and identified improving work morale as its number one strategic priority for the new fiscal year. The leadership team decided to launch a company-wide training in which they focused on three objectives: promoting a workplace environment that valued work–life balance, opening up lines of communication between managers and their direct reports, and making New Brands a place where people wanted to work.

Managers attended a two-day retreat in which they practiced giving and getting feedback to and from their reports. Management also practiced leading difficult conversations. At the end of the two days, the leadership at NewBrands was excited to create real and lasting change. Unfortunately, after all the intensive practice on multiple fronts, the improvements they had pinned their hopes on didn't materialize. So much work and nothing to show for it. Why? Had they practiced the wrong skills? Had they not practiced enough? Were the role plays, the feedback, not well executed? The answer to all of those questions is a resounding no.

The problem wasn't what or even how they practiced. The problem was what happened after the practice: the managers went back to their old ways. They had learned new skills through practice but were not held accountable for the implementation of key skills they had practiced. During the retreat, managers were observed during role plays practicing ways to communicate better with their direct reports. They received and acted on feedback. And that was the end of it. When it came time to take these skills into their real world of work, no one was there to observe them.

After this failed experience in bringing new skills to his company, Brad, a young NewBrands executive, realized that drive-by trainings wouldn't work. He set about to embed the practice of new skills into their trainings, and he was relentless in planning how to follow-up after practice in order to actually change behavior. He started by simply observing and giving feedback on the new skills in performance. During meetings, he found subtle ways to cue employees to remind them of the work they had done in practice. He did this by creating posters of the principles they had trained in and practiced, which allowed him to signal people during performance. And finally, he measured the effectiveness of their trainings by collecting data from his employees: surveys on how particular skills were being used and how often they were being coached on key skills by their managers. In essence, Brad brought as much intentionality to the follow-up done after practice as he gave to planning the practice itself.

In trying to improve performance, one of the biggest mistakes that leaders and managers make is neglecting to follow up in strategic and thoughtful ways in order to make new initiatives or trainings "stick," a term popularized by the Heath brothers in their book *Made to Stick*. Chip and Dan Heath mostly focus on making *ideas* stick—so they will be "understood and remembered, and have a lasting impact." In this chapter we will focus on discrete skills and how to make those skills stick and endure to become habits.

At countless companies and organizations, a lot of time and money are invested in improvement plans and training materials, yet all too little attention is given to how behavior is actually changing once the training is over and the dust has settled. We often expect the fruits of our labor to immediately come alive—whether we're in a classroom or in a boardroom—with no clear and consistent follow-up. One of the most compelling (and discouraging) examples of this comes from a study done by the U.S. Department of Education which found that even though we have more than doubled the amount we spend per student in American public schools, reading scores in middle school have remained flat and in high school they have actually declined.[1] This could be due to the vicious cycle of new initiatives and trainings and workshops (and money invested), which then fall into the same trap. What you do as a leader after practicing new skills can be just as important as the practice itself, as it helps the takeaways from practice to stick and ensures that practice translates into improved performance over time. Read on for how to make practice "stick."

RULE 38
LOOK FOR THE RIGHT THINGS

After practicing a skill, we must observe and provide feedback on the skill in actual performance as well. The rules of feedback in practice outlined in the chapter on feedback still apply: shorten the feedback loop, practice using the feedback, use positive feedback, and check for understanding of the feedback. These rules also apply in the feedback that we deliver during performance. When we talk about "looking for the right things," we are referring to the observation and feedback that we give during the performance— post-practice. Stated most simply, if you want something to get done, measure it. And the simplest way to measure it is to observe it.

A vice president of sales may have her account executives practice their sales pitches focusing on one particular skill (Rule 10), such as clearly describing the product in comparison to the competition, or summarizing the presentation with conviction. The VP will give feedback on the pitch, then have account execs integrate that feedback (Rule 23). But post-practice, when the real game has begun and account execs are delivering their pitches to real, prospective clients, the VP needs to observe the actual performance and provide specific feedback on the aspects of the pitch that were isolated during practice. The key is looking for the right things. This shows the account execs that what they practiced matters. They will be more likely to learn the skills and have them "stick" because they were expected to use them.

There is so much to look for. How do you know where to begin? Your best point of reference is to look back to what you practiced. One way to do this effectively is to create an observation tool or template specifically aligned with the skills you've practiced so that both leaders and performers know what to focus on during performance. For example, when practicing with "Cold Call"—a teaching technique frequently used in law schools (and successful middle, elementary, and high schools), in which the teacher calls on a student whether or not his or her hand is raised—one school we know follows up trainings with classroom observations that focus on the specific skills in Cold Calling. These observations focus on the finer points of the technique; for example, the point when the student's name is called (before or after asking the question), whether the technique is expected (students aren't caught off guard because they expect it to be used), and whether it is scaffolded (questions start easier and get harder throughout a particular questioning sequence). Aligning observations in such a targeted way allows leaders to make sure that teachers are Cold Calling; it also gives teachers specific feedback on how to use the technique effectively.

Applying this idea in other settings, you could build a rubric that lists the concrete skills you want people to demonstrate during performance. You'd use it first in practice (for example, the patient checklist in the "standardized patient encounter" at Cornell); then, in post-practice, the rubric would support the targeted observation and evaluation of skills in performance. You could then aggregate the data to help you know what skills you need to practice more.

Narrowing and aligning observations post-practice allows you to get beyond the basics faster and more efficiently, and can lead to lasting change in behavior. In addition to having teachers practice Cold Calling before using it in the classroom, we also have leaders practice *observing* for Cold Call in the classroom. In our workshops, we ask school leaders to watch videos of teachers using Cold Call, and they use an observation template that lists the key skills involved in effective Cold Calling. This helps them to practice looking for the finer points of Cold Calling. In order to help skills stick post-practice, not only should performers practice in advance, but leaders should also practice observing for key skills that need to stick.

You can take your aligned observations up a notch by also making them transparent and predictable to performers. Tell your players, "As I watch you teach [play; operate; perform] today, I'll be looking to see how you're doing with redirecting off-task behavior [receiving the ball with a "W" hand structure; using the correct stitches as you close the wound; clearly articulating the notes in your scales]." Predictable observation allows performers to proactively work towards a goal. They know what you are looking for and can hold themselves accountable merely by your presence during their performance. You no longer have to remind anyone to try a new technique, a request that can feel insincere when there is no accountability mechanism. The act of observing reminds performers in an open and honest way that you will be looking for the things you pratice during performance.

Here's how the whole process of aligning observation comes together at our best schools. First, observations are such a given part of what our principals do that all teachers expect their leaders to be in their classroom on a consistent basis to observe for the techniques they have been practicing. Leaders may use an observation tool like the one we describe above, or they may simply let teachers know that they'll be coming by for the next two weeks looking for a particular skill that has been practiced. They often do not use an actual rubric, but teachers know in advance what they should be working on. This lets the feedback continue to phase through discrete skills naturally and efficiently even after the teachers' application of feedback has moved from practice to performance. It also holds our teachers accountable (in a positive and supportive way) for trying what they've learned. This predictability also leads to a shared investment in success. Leaders and teachers are working in cooperation with a mutual intention to improve, which allows teachers to engage in further real-world practice.

Managers can't be everywhere at once, observing all skills at all times. This is where video becomes a useful tool as you invest your players in looking for the right things in their own performance. Asking your employees to videotape themselves in performance helps invest them in their own development. Ask them to record five minutes of a particular performance (a presentation, a sales pitch, a deposition, a math lesson, a college seminar); then ask them to reflect on their execution of particular skills. What did they try? What was challenging? What was surprising? Observation isn't just about looking for success; it's also about looking for challenges and ways to support people in those challenges. You want people to be comfortable exposing error (Rule 31): ask people to submit video of their trying out a new skill during performance. This allows you to help skills stick, because people are held accountable for using them, and it encourages a dialogue on how to ensure the skills are used effectively in the face of challenges.

In the previous chapter we discussed goal-setting and mutual commitments as a way of building a culture of practice. Applying these ideas post-practice can also help tailor your observations to align with the goals your players and performers have set. Post-practice, ask participants to reflect (in writing or in a meeting) on what they learned from the practice and the specific skills they are going to focus on in their own performance. Your observations can then focus on the specific goals that individuals have set for themselves. This will increase your accountability to each other, to your shared organizational goals, and to a culture of practice.

Look for the Right Things
- After isolating skills during practice, observe people during the actual performance in order to provide feedback on the discrete skills that were practiced.
- Create an observation tool to use during performance that is aligned to the skills you have practiced.
- Allow leaders to practice observing for discrete skills during the performance.

- If you are going to evaluate a particular skill in performance, allow performers to practice the skill first.
- Post-practice, ask performers to set their own discrete goals for performance, and then observe them for the skills required to achieve those goals.

RULE 39
COACH DURING THE GAME
(DON'T TEACH)

Coaching during a game can be helpful, but *teaching* during a game is distracting and counterproductive. You can't learn and perform at the same time. Practice builds unconscious and automatic skills. Trying to teach during a game disrupts this process. The coaching that you do during a game should only reinforce, with reminders, what has been taught in practice. Teach, then, during practice; during the game, remind with short, positive phrases that tell players what they should do.

Practice provides a space for coaching to occur without the high stakes of the performance. In professional tennis, it is illegal to receive any coaching (or teaching) during a tennis match at the majors. This is a long-standing rule that distinguishes tennis from other professional sports. It is one of the game's most unusual and controversial rules, celebrated by traditionalists but also hotly debated. There have been many instances in which players were suspected of receiving illegal outside coaching. The most notorious was at the 2006 US Open when Maria Sharapova's father held up a banana in an effort to remind her to eat. In effect, her father was coaching: sending a visual reminder to her to eat. In some of our schools, teacher coaches use a similar strategy. They stand in the back of the class with two colored note cards: a red card might remind a teacher to call on a student with a hand raised, and a yellow card might signal the teacher to ask the class to respond chorally. These reminders reflect the skills that the teacher has been practicing; they are not teaching new skills during the game.

Lee Canter, author of *Assertive Discipline*, has taken this idea of coaching during the game to a whole other level. Canter has trained thousands of teachers in effective classroom management techniques. Most recently, he has incorporated an additional coaching element to his repertoire: Real-Time Coaching. In this method, Canter works with teachers using a wireless device, a "bug in the ear," so that he can coach teachers *while* they are teaching. This untraditional method is sometimes met with skepticism and fear, yet it should be noted that he isn't actually teaching teachers anything *new* while they are teaching. Instead, he is coaching teachers on what he has already taught them during practice. His framework on behavior management is simple: give students clear directions; narrate the positive ("Jeremiah is working silently"); calmly and firmly correct off-task students. Canter teaches these principles to his teachers, then he has them practice these skills. Post-practice, he sets off to see his teachers in the classroom.

Canter gives teachers just three simple cues while they are teaching, all of which refer back to the discrete skills teachers practiced. He may say, "Give clear directions," "Narrate Joshua," or "Correct Sienna," simple prompts that remind teachers about what they learned and practiced in his workshops. When asked about the effectiveness of this approach, a teacher is quoted on Michael Goldstein's "Starting an Ed School" blog as saying, "Unbelievable. I knew it, I knew all that stuff, I learned it all last year. But somehow it never clicked like it did when Lee was telling me what to do, right in front of the kids. Totally worked."[2]

How might this idea play itself out in a different context? Let's take a task that many leaders have to conquer: public speaking. It is widely known that public speaking is the number one fear reported by people in the United States, ranking even above the fear of death.[3] The best way to conquer this fear is through preparation and practice. A lot of us think that we can practice speeches by ourselves in front of a mirror or to an empty room, sometimes only reading the words softly to ourselves. While any preparation is better than none, the best way to practice delivering a speech or presentation to an audience (and therefore to conquer your fears) is to actually have an audience and to approach the presentation the same way you would in the game (Rule 12). This can be an audience of one, but it is important to practice in front of someone. And ideally, the person that you practice with will be someone who will be in the audience during the actual presentation.

As our team prepares for workshops, we present our sections in front of each other and give each other feedback. We may coach each other on our content as well as how we deliver it. Then, during our workshops (post-practice, during the big game), we can continue to build on the feedback and coaching we've given each other during practice. At our workshops, you will frequently find one of us in the back of the room giving nonverbal signals to the presenter (we usually present in a team of two or three, alternating portions of the workshop between us). For example, Erica is working on speaking more slowly, improving her posture, and circulating around the room less in order to command more presence. We have signals for each of these skills that we have built during practice. When we deliver these signals to Erica during the workshop, they are easy for her to incorporate without disrupting the flow of her content or confusing her ability to facilitate practice. If we hadn't practiced ahead of time, it would be challenging, distracting, and detrimental to her performance to be taught new skills during the workshop.

Coach During the Game (Don't Teach)

- You can't teach new things during a game or a performance. It only confuses performers.
- During the performance (post-practice) you should only coach on those skills that have already been taught during practice.
- Coaching during the game should only cue and remind people to use what they have learned.

RULE 40
KEEP TALKING

In baseball, the first and third base coaches communicate quickly, effectively, and efficiently with their players and other coaches using discrete hand signals that tell batters and runners exactly what to do. They may signal to steal a base, bunt, lead off a base in a certain way, sacrifice, take a pitch without swinging, and countless other strategic moves. They do this all without words. Without the common language created by these base signals quickly shared between coaches and players, games that have been won might otherwise have been lost, with fewer runs scored, fewer bases stolen, and fewer hits sacrificed. Having a common language like this is equally vital to the success of organizations that practice.

When you have your players practice and master a new skill, it is important to give that skill a name so people know what it is they've learned (Rule 11). After building your common vocabulary, how do you keep it alive post-practice? Doug's son the soccer player knows a Cruyff Turn from a Drag Back from a V-Cut. This means that he and his coach can talk clearly about how he used them (or might have used them) in a game. It allows him to be coached on what he has mastered in practice. Similarly, surgeons know a simple interrupted stitch from a continuous stitch from a horizontal mattress stitch. Developing this shared vocabulary and using it post-practice allows surgeons to discuss and develop their technique quickly with one another. If there weren't different names, the different methods and skills would ultimately blend into one. Naming skills, techniques, strategies, and approaches makes them come alive in the operating room, the soccer field, the boardroom, the classroom, and even your living room. Use your common language during practice to develop skills, and continue to use it post-practice to make those skills stick. In our workshops, when participants analyze video of teachers demonstrating a technique, we also ask that they practice using the vocabulary we have just taught. This helps establish the expectation that it's important to use the common language, both in practice and in discussion of practice.

Once the common language has been established in practice, it is important to maintain an ongoing conversation about what you have practiced in as many different ways as you can. For example, two colleagues may follow up practice informally: "I was thinking about our practice on market strategy. I think we should try to implement a strategic product road map for this account." Or a principal may e-mail her whole staff to highlight individuals who are implementing new techniques right away: "I saw Hillary use Precise Praise in class today, and she taught me something by strategically choosing the students in the class to praise based on where they were sitting. A student at every table was praised for an aspect of their work, so all students in the class had a model to work from." Using the common language post-practice focuses on and solidifies the skills that have been practiced.

"Transaction cost" is the amount of resources that it takes to execute an exchange, be it economic, verbal, or something else.[4] Developing a shared vocabulary reduces the transaction cost for peer–peer discussion (between surgeons), as well as leader–peer discussion (father–son, coach–player, manager–employee); it also builds culture, because you belong to something with a language of its own. In the example of the first base coach, low transaction costs are vital: batters and runners do not have time to discuss their strategy; they need to have a way of communicating in less than five seconds before the pitcher delivers his pitch. Low transaction costs are equally vital in any organization with a bottom line. While you want to keep transaction costs low during practice in order to maximize the time actually spent practicing, it's important to keep them low in post-practice as well. Using a shared vocabulary during performance is a very efficient and low-cost way to help skills stick.

In a recent editorial in the *Wall Street Journal*, Coach Mike Krzyzewski, who has led the Duke Men's Basketball team to four

NCAA championships and eleven Final Fours (tying for the second most in college basketball history), writes: "I believe that my work is as much about words as it is about basketball. Choosing the right words is no less important to the outcome of a game than choosing the right players and strategies for the court."[5] He discusses the importance of motivating his players through "vivid stories" to help them believe in themselves. Coach K frequently draws on the experiences of friends, family, and former team members who showed willpower, dependability, and courage. These stories are invaluable in helping to connect with and inspire his players. "When an audience makes these associations," Krzyzewski continues, "we have found common ground. We are no longer merely exchanging words; we are being mutually motivated by their meaning."[6] Words can be teaching tools, and they can inspire. They allow you to teach new things during practice and draw on them for your team during the game with low transaction costs. A shared vocabulary wins games, inspires teachers, steals bases, and brings people together. It keeps the benefits of practice alive, long after the practice is over.

Keep Talking

- Name the discrete skills and drills that you practice.
- Use these names to discuss skills and their application post-practice in order to keep them alive in your organization.

RULE 41
WALK THE LINE (BETWEEN SUPPORT AND DEMAND)

Once the game has begun and the opportunity to practice has ended (temporarily), the stakes are—in some ways—higher. Coaches have to support their players and performers and keep them progressing in the face of failures that no longer feel small and harmless. At the same time, coaches have to continue to demand excellent performance, with a sense of urgency fitting the importance of each performance.

At Uncommon Schools, our teachers return for professional development three weeks prior to the beginning of the school year. We devote a lot of time during these three weeks to practice: teaching mock lessons, participating in small practice drills, role-playing conversations with families, practicing lesson planning with feedback from colleagues. Once our summer trainings end, we often feel a small shift in the dynamics between teachers and leaders. With the intense practice of the summer behind us, the stakes are raised, and our excited and invigorated staffs become overwhelmed (yet remain energized) by the looming, daunting task of teaching real students. It is in these times that the principles of practice become that much more important. Practice has to be a judgment-free zone where there are no repercussions for failure: feedback is given and implemented, but it still feels safe. Teachers don't have 30 kindergarteners in front of them or mountains of papers to grade or assessments to analyze—yet. But part of the understanding of practice, especially this practice in advance of the school year, is that when it's game time, everybody has to deliver.

As a leader, one of the most difficult and important roles you play is the evaluator. As the evaluator, you have to tell your players whether they're good enough, if they are starters or on the bench, and what specifically they need to work on. Leaders must be transparent about playing their demand and support roles simultaneously from the outset. As a leader it would be disingenuous if you only claimed to make people better through support. Several years ago, before coming to Uncommon Schools, Katie had a teacher who was struggling in the classroom. As she tells it, when she gave him difficult feedback one day, she then asked what his thoughts were. His response was, "Give me a warning before you fire me." In looking back at this moment, Katie realized that she hadn't played it right. Her reply to him had been, "I'm going to coach you." In thinking about the line between support and demand, Katie wishes that she had said, "I want you to succeed, and I'm going to do my best to support you in that. I'm not ready to talk to you about your leaving the organization. It may get to that point, but let's keep trying and practicing before we talk about anybody getting fired." This type of response would have communicated her support, but it also would have communicated that ultimately she was his evaluator and would have to act accordingly if his poor performance continued. Her supportiveness didn't remove her responsibility and commitment to the success of the students. She had to walk the line between support and demand.

Leaders who walk this line well consistently recognize and reward hard work, but they also provide specific feedback when performance doesn't meet particular standards; when necessary they communicate it with a sense of urgency. Consistently echoing the mission of an organization is a useful tool when enforcing performance standards. It's important to hold people to these standards both in practice and in the game, and to be transparent about the roles that you play as coach and as evaluator.

How do you walk the line to ensure that practice sticks? Think back to Susan and David's interactions in the chapter on feedback. Susan often experienced David's feedback as "advice" rather than guidance that she needed to implement. The dynamic that existed between Susan and David was David's responsibility as the leader. He needed to more clearly frame his feedback (and his role as supervisor) not as a suggestion but as something required of her to improve her performance. When you effectively walk the line between support and demand, it improves performance and it preserves relationships. You and your players are clear about expectations for performance, and players better understand your role in their development.

Walk the Line (Between Support and Demand)

- When the game (post-practice) has begun, be transparent about your role as evaluator.
- Reward hard work and communicate a sense of urgency when improvement is necessary.
- Post-practice, frame feedback not as helpful advice but as something required to improve performance.

RULE 42
MEASURE SUCCESS

In his book *Better*, Atul Gawande shares the story of Virginia Apgar, whose development of the Apgar score, a quick and simple measurement of newborn health, had a tremendous impact on infant mortality rates. In the 1930s, one in 30 children died at birth, showing very little improvement from the same statistics an entire century earlier. The creation of the Apgar score allowed doctors and nurses to quickly and effectively evaluate the health of newborns from the moment of their birth, and it is a measure that continues today. Babies receive a score for their coloring, their pulse, their reflexes, their muscle tone, and their breathing, at one minute and again at five minutes after birth. The simple existence of this measure allowed doctors to systematically collect data that had previously not been used. Gawande describes the impact of this measurement:

> The score turned an intangible and impressionistic clinical concept—the condition of new babies—into numbers that people could collect and compare. Using it required more careful observation and documentation of the true condition of every baby. . . . It quickly became clear that a baby with a terrible Apgar score at one minute could often be resuscitated—with measures like oxygen and warming—to an

excellent score at five minutes. Neonatal intensive care units sprang into existence. The score also began to alter how childbirth itself was managed.[7]

The Apgar score has saved millions of children's lives since its creation in 1953. Measurements drive results in the classroom, in the operating room, on the basketball court, and in the board-room. Therefore, once practice is in place, measure its effectiveness post-practice. You should measure two things:

1 *The effectiveness of your practice.* Does doing something in practice actually enable people to do it in performance?
2. *Practicing the right things.* Are you practicing the things that need to be practiced in order to improve performance?

The typical coach will often watch a game as an unfolding narrative. Coaches may look back at a game and have a general idea of how it went: "We played well." "We struggled to play together as a team." "We had trouble on defense." But to determine what it is that you should be practicing, you should look at games (or lessons, surgeries, or sales pitches) as a series of data points. Instead of subjectively evaluating how your team played, look for specific data that reflect the skills you have practiced. For example, how many players made diagonal runs? How many teachers asked their students to do something again if they didn't have 100% participation? How many times did a particular sales strategy result in a sale?

Collecting and measuring data on performance post-practice allows you to evaluate your own effectiveness in facilitating practice. Back in the chapter "How to Practice" you read about high school basketball coach Bill Resler, who obsessively analyzed game tapes to determine the specific skills his players needed to focus on during practice. When skills didn't stick in the game, he assessed why and then built his findings into future practices.

In looking back at his work with teachers, which formed the basis for *Teach Like a Champion*, Doug reflects that the only thing he knows for sure is that some of it must have been wrong. Maybe he was attending to a particular aspect of a teacher's instruction, like her ability to give clear directions (the technique "What to Do"), when a teacher did something else that actually drove her instruction—and the strong results in her classroom. As we now use the techniques from *Teach Like a Champion* to train other teachers, we are starting to use data to measure how the techniques are impacting student performance data. When we train teachers using these techniques, we have begun to ask ourselves questions to evaluate our own success. Is student data changing as a result of this work; that is, are these techniques, which we believe make teachers effective, resulting in improved student performance? Which techniques have the strongest impact on student achievement? In asking these questions, we are both measuring and ensuring our success. We respond by adapting our practice-laden workshops to the data as we gather and evaluate it.

In our work we have found that it is not enough to measure success simply through self-reporting after a practice workshop. For one thing, self-reporting is notoriously unreliable. For another, gathering this type of data during practice doesn't allow us to determine the efficacy of the practice, because we aren't actually seeing the practice translate to performance. We therefore have started using other measures at different intervals following a workshop to ensure that practice with our techniques "sticks." We have started to implement site visits and the exchange of video. Are the techniques we teach alive and well in the classroom one month following our workshops? Six months? The following school year? If so, why? If not, why not? Was it because of ineffective practice or inadequate support in implementation? And when techniques are thriving in a classroom, are student data positively impacted?

In order to guarantee that practice will drive success, measure the impact of the practice. This will help you to refine your practice as well as know whether you are practicing the right skills.

Measure Success

- Use performance as a series of data points to evaluate the effectiveness of practice and to drive what is practiced in the future.
- Use multiple methods to gather this data (self-reporting, observation and evaluation, performance metrics).

The follow-up that you do post-practice will ensure that the skills you practice will be lasting. Let's take a look back at NewBrands. What errors did they make that resulted in skills not sticking following their practice? First, skills were not observed for, nor were they evaluated. This communicated to employees that the skills they had practiced were not valued. Leadership (and therefore the rest of the company) didn't continue to use the common language that they started building in practice, so the discrete skills and principles didn't remain an integral part of the dialogue. And lastly, leaders didn't attempt to measure the impact of their practice. Without these key action steps, the chips were stacked against them. Use the rules outlined in this chapter: once you have integrated practice into how you develop talent, follow up post-practice to ensure that skills stick and that behaviors really change.

CONCLUSION

The Monday Morning Test

When we lead our workshops, we strive to make the techniques we teach and practice pass the "Monday Morning Test." The guidance we give has to be specific and concrete enough for teachers to be able to use it productively first thing on Monday morning. The key to passing the Monday Morning Test is not lofty ideals but specific actions that can be immediately implemented. We hope that if you are a coach or a trainer or already engage in regular, intentional practice, specific practical applications for the ideas in this book are already obvious. What if you are a partner in a law firm, the head of a division or a non-profit agency, the principal of a school, a manager at a grocery store, or an individual seeking to improve at something you have not regularly practiced before? What are the first steps in bringing the power of practice to your profession, your organization, or your life? How do you begin to get better at getting better?

The pages that follow are an effort to help you think about application and implementation. Here are concrete actions and approaches that can be applied in an array of settings and that you can start using as early as Monday morning. We describe three scenarios of what it could look like to put our rules into action. The first scenario describes how you might apply these rules as a leader or manager in your organization. The second scenario looks at how the rules could apply when you are working one-on-one with a colleague, mentee, or small group of people. And the final scenario suggests how you might use these rules as an individual in the quest for success in your field or endeavor.

MONDAY MORNING FOR ORGANIZATIONS

If you are a leader or member in an organization and want to bring the power of practice to how you develop and improve people, the following rules can be used first thing on Monday morning.

Rule 2: Practice the 20
Use this rule to identify a handful of the most important skills that you need individuals in your organization to master in order to drive 80 percent of your results. If you don't know where to start in identifying those skills that apply to your work, then use another concept from this same rule and leverage the wisdom of crowds. Poll your people (draft the e-mail first thing on Monday morning) and ask them to respond to the following question by three o'clock in the afternoon: "What are the three most important skills we all need to have in order to be successful?" It's not an exact science, but you will get a pretty good starting point for what you need to practice, and further, your team will be invested in the process. Depending on your company or organization's size, you will get a variety of responses and can narrow in on the top three skills to practice.

Rule 10: Isolate the Skill
Let's say the top skill that your organization recognizes is the need to "effectively communicate with clients." It is now your leadership team's job to break down this larger skill into isolated skills for practice. What managerial skills are most necessary for success?

What skills do you most need to isolate in order to "effectively communicate with clients"? Maybe it means isolating skills like using eye contact, narrowing the focus of presentations, or active listening by nodding and taking notes. Make sure the skills that you isolate are small enough to be intentionally practiced.

Rule 11: Name It

Give each skill a sticky name that will mean something to everybody in your organization. When something becomes an "it," you can talk about it, model it, practice it, and give feedback on it. What skills or concepts will you name so that they can be taught and practiced?

Rule 16: Call Your Shots

You have the right skills in your sights and you have them named; now as the leader it's time to call your shots. You should model not only the skill itself but your willingness to practice in front of others and to ask for feedback. Tell your team what you're working on—for example, active listening—and how you're going to demonstrate it in meetings or in a role play with a "client." Ask people for feedback on the skill; then model how you practice again while integrating the feedback (notice here that we're also inserting Rule 23, "Practice *Using* Feedback").

Beyond Monday Morning

We recognize that large, sweeping organizational change cannot be created in one day. Use the rules in the following discussion to continue on your path to improving practice within your organization.

If practice is new to your organization, you will be best served if you anticipate people's potential resistance to it (Rule 32, "Break Down the Barriers to Practice"). Modeling your own willingness to practice will certainly help. It will also help if you anticipate the different reasons that people in your organization may be hesitant to engage in practice, as well as anticipate particular individuals who may be especially resistant. Maybe the public aspect of practice will be particularly challenging for some; if that's the case, then allow them to practice privately first. Others may be skeptical of or resistant to change. Ask these individuals to trust the process and to give you feedback afterwards on what worked for them in practice and what was challenging. Then continue to break down barriers through continued practice. Whatever the barriers may be, anticipate them so that you are ready to lead your team in overcoming them. And be on the lookout for creative ways for avoiding practice, like we saw in Rule 32.

In addition, when you first incorporate the exchange of feedback between colleagues in practice, you may want to use Rule 28, "Make It an Everyday Thing," and provide sentence starters such as, "I liked how you . . . " and "Next time you should try . . . " Make it clear that feedback (through modeling and explicit guidance) has to be precise (focused on replicable actions). You have to get past nice: don't be afraid to give genuine feedback in the name of organizational improvement.

Finally, don't lose sight of the objective of your practice, and find creative ways to make it fun so that people will be excited to engage in it. Use friendly competitions between departments and cheer for each other during practice; you will see an outpouring of peer support and teamwork during actual performance as well.

MONDAY MORNING FOR A MENTEE OR SMALL TEAM

In a recent *New York Times* article, "What They Don't Teach Law Students: Lawyering," David Segal describes the lack of practical legal training that students receive in law school. This fact contributes to additional legal fees that clients end up paying for through the on-the-job training of young attorneys; it has led to a steep decline in the number of students being hired straight out of law school, and calls into question the preparation that law schools across the country give to their students.

In the article, Segal quotes the general counsel of a major corporation who describes the problem: "The fundamental issue is that law schools are producing people who are not capable of being counselors. They are lawyers in the sense that they have law degrees, but they aren't ready to be a provider of services."[1] Segal points out that one of the first-year requirements in law school is Contracts, a course in which students examine historic landmark cases. But what students don't learn in most Contracts classes is how to go through the process of drafting a contract that both parties will agree to, a skill that almost all lawyers have to have on the job.

To address this practical preparation and skills gap, law firms (or even the law schools themselves) could follow the sequence of rules laid out above for organizations. One such law firm, Drinker Biddle, with offices in eight states and two countries, has created a four-month program for new associates to prepare them for the on-the-job challenges and skills required of them in corporate law. A graduate of the program, Dennis P. O'Reilly, says of the program, "What they taught us at this law firm is how to be a lawyer. What they taught us at law school is how to graduate from law school."[2]

The law profession is not alone in underutilizing the power of practice to prepare professionals for the demands that on-the-job performance requires. Working with a small team or even with one individual within your firm or company, you can start to bring practice to help with preparation and performance. For lawyers practicing contract writing, you might also have them practice how to speak to a non-lawyer about what a contract means. This concept could be applied in all professions. Doctors need to learn how to explain medical decisions to their patients; IT specialists need to know how to explain concepts to technophobes; teachers need to be able to interpret assessment results for parents. All professions could practice translating for novices in order to address the age-old problem described by George Bernard Shaw:

"All professions are conspiracies against the laity." Practice explaining technical terms that are unique to your profession in order to better serve your profession and your field.

Maybe you don't work in the context of a larger organization (you may be a writer, an artist, or a coach of an individual sport), or perhaps you work in a larger organization but are only responsible for a small team (as an art director at an ad agency, or a board member of a local sports league). Perhaps you lead a large organization but want to start small in using practice to transform your organization. In any of these cases you may find it useful to apply the following rules to your work, and you can start first thing Monday morning. Begin with one person, one skill, 15 minutes every week. Use the following rules to get you going.

Rule 7: Differentiate Drill from Scrimmage

Differentiate drill from scrimmage and you will be able to bring your practice to a whole new level. Learn from Weill Cornell Medical School and present your team with discrete drills that isolate the skills your team will need to use in performance. To prepare attorneys for a deposition, have associates practice asking their five key questions, whose answers will help them win the deposition (keeping the case from going to court), rather than having them scrimmage and go through their entire list of questions. Or perhaps you work with associates who will never see the inside of a courtroom. Have them practice how to communicate with conviction with another party who is not aligned with their interests and then reach an agreement that is advantageous and acceptable to both parties.

You don't work at a law firm? Apply this rule with your mentees or your own small team. If you want to incorporate daily practice, you can learn from Nikki and Maggie, back in the Introduction. With a colleague, practice, say, the opening and concluding remarks of your presentation in which you will request funding for your next project. Focus on discrete skills, one at a time. Don't rush to scrimmage because it's easier; focus on the smaller practice tasks that will more likely lead to success in the performance. Incorporate practice drills for 15 minutes a day, or take one hour a week for feedback and practice.

Rule 23: Practice *Using* Feedback (Not Just Getting It)

Giving feedback to those you supervise may not be new to you and your team. But bring your feedback process to your *practice* sessions and then ask for your mentee or players to use feedback immediately. When you see them practice using it, you will observe if (1) your feedback is clear, (2) they are able to use it, and (3) your feedback results in improved performance. Use the principles from the feedback chapter to keep your feedback focused on what to do differently in the future rather than on what was done wrong in the past (Rule 8, "Correct Instead of Critique"). Then ask your players to incorporate the feedback.

Rule 14: Make Each Minute Matter

In the world of billable hours (or at any company with a bottom line), time is money. The more time that your associates have in their day to be billing clients, the stronger the firm will be. The more efficient your small marketing team is, the more clients you will be able to reach. But when faced with first-year associates or account managers who are not prepared for the demands of the job, you will have to train them. Create systems to enable your practices to be urgent, tight, and efficient. Use timers and structured protocols to allow as many people the chance to practice and use feedback as possible, or to allow one person multiple takes.

Rule 22: Get Ready for Your Close-up

In your quick drills, videotape each other (a simple video from your smartphone will do). Have your mentees watch the video, reflect on their execution of the technique, and then practice again, incorporating the changes they want to make.

MONDAY MORNING FOR YOURSELF

Many of us—the would-be superstars or closet virtuosos—may not have the privilege of practicing with a team. Or perhaps we are an anonymous, small cog in an organizational behemoth. Practice still has its place. And you can use several rules in this book, first thing on Monday morning, to achieve success through practice.

Javier Bardem was featured in a recent *New York Times* piece that traced his career, describing the performances that have set him apart from the merely mediocre. Bardem has won not only an Academy Award but also a Golden Globe Award, a SAG, and countless awards in Europe.[3] Every colleague quoted in the article commented on Bardem's consistently outstanding performances, but they focused mostly on his hard work and consistent practice. One of the directors he has worked with, Julian Schnabel, observed, "I think the best actors are those who are not only talented, but work harder than anybody else, and that's Javy."

The article traces Bardem's talent back to his childhood and the hours he spent helping his mother, an actress, review her lines and practice her roles. Watching his mother relentlessly go over and over her lines until she knew them cold, and only then seeing her develop her character, framed for him what would become his personal work ethic and habits that would produce consistently excellent results (Rule 21, "Model the Path"). He reflects, "To get to the art, one must work very hard. Art doesn't exist just as talent. It exists as effort, work and judgment." We believe that the same can be said for teaching and for most if not all performance professions. The top performers are those who continue to strive, grow, and develop—in other words, they continue to practice.

Despite Bardem's wild success and his consistent offers of interesting roles from high-profile directors who have great confidence in his abilities, he continues to work with an acting coach, Juan Carlos Corazza. The article explains, "They have worked together nearly 20 years, since the beginning of Mr. Bardem's career. In a telephone interview from Madrid, where he lives, Mr. Corazza said that Mr. Bardem not only consults with him as he prepares for each role but also attends his classes and workshops, where he is sometimes matched with beginning actors."

Learning from the greats like actor Javier Bardem, surgeon Atul Gawande, and soccer phenomenon Lionel Messi, we outline here the rules that you as an individual can apply to improve your intentional use of practice in order to become a star in your own profession or pastime.

Rule 17: ~~Make Models Believable~~ Seek Believable Models

We are slightly altering the use of this rule here. As an individual you need to seek out believable models, people who are doing the same work you are doing, in a similar context. Further, you need to try to understand, as Bardem did with his mother, how they *practice*. Don't just go to the symphony to hear the greats perform; go behind the scenes and watch how they practice—the process by which they get better. You don't have to live near a concert hall to be able to do this. YouTube is an amazing tool for practice. Use it to see how the greats practice. On Monday morning, enter "Itzhak Perlman Practicing" into their search tool and see what you find.

Rule 23: [Seek and] Practice *Using* Feedback

Learn from Atul Gawande and seek out a coach. It doesn't have to cost you anything. Ask someone, even a peer or colleague in your field, to be your "extra ear." Practice using the feedback you receive from your coach. Don't just nod your head in acceptance; immediately try out your coach's suggestions to incorporate them into your practice. This will make you more likely to apply the feedback during your performance as well.

Rule 4: Unlock Creativity

Identify those skills in your profession or hobby that are weak, thus preventing you from being more creative. Practice these skills again and again until they are committed to your muscle memory. This will allow you to free up more creative space and reach new heights, whether you are sitting at a piano, delivering a speech in a boardroom, or teaching math to 30 sixth-graders.

Rule 31: Normalize Error
Learn from our skier friend and the typist in the chapter on culture. Be willing to push yourself a little bit harder, out of your comfort zone, and take calculated risks in the name of improvement. Maybe that means practicing a difficult conversation that you never thought you could have with your boss about your career development, speaking with conviction and persuasion. Or perhaps it means practicing your violin solo with the metronome four ticks higher than you normally would. Push yourself to make mistakes in the name of improvement.

■ ■ ■

Use practice to help you or your organization pass your own Monday Morning Test. Use this plug-and-play combination of rules to start you on your way. You will no doubt find other ways to put the ideas from this book into action immediately. The key is to dive in, take one small step, and then keep going.

FINAL WORDS ON PRACTICE

The past few years have been dramatic and often stressful for teachers, much as they have been stressful for other professionals as well. As the expectations increase for schools to demonstrate unequivocally that students are learning, so does the pressure for more rigorous evaluation of teachers—and sometimes even more public evaluation of teachers, whose scores in some cities are now published in the newspaper. While it is right that schools and teachers be accountable for results, many teachers are rightly frustrated by the lack of equivalent support they receive in seeking success. What do we conclude if we believe—not as some have suggested, that teachers are lazy and indifferent—that teachers are a committed, hard-working, effective group of people who do incredibly difficult work with little recompense or appreciation? What if teachers working under these conditions have mediocre results and urgently want to get better, but their schools or districts fail to make them better? What if they are good but want to be great and, again, are not supported? What if they are great and want to be life-changing?

In the education sector, we argue that it is the fundamental obligation of organizations to make people better. At the very least it is an opportunity, one of incredible magnitude as the work we do throughout the economy is exposed to more and more competition. What was once a local competition is now global and has become more and more reliant on "knowledge workers." The capacity to develop people and make them better is, you could argue, the best measure of an organization's worth. And yet most organizations, including educational organizations, ironically, fail to leverage some of the most basic, effective, and straightforward tools that could help them in that struggle—in part perhaps because they appear so basic and straightforward. (We hope to have demonstrated in this book that while they are powerful, they are not simple.)

In 14th-century England, a Franciscan friar named William of Ockham observed that when there are competing possible explanations for an occurrence and no preponderance of data points to favor one or another, it makes sense to choose the simplest possible explanation, as it is more likely to be true. This observation, known today as Occam's Razor, can be applied to a great many of our struggles in the field of developing people.

For example, what is the best explanation for the fact that students don't achieve in all classrooms? It could be that we need to rethink the tenets of teaching and discover new principles to inform what we do, but it could more simply be that when we do know effective methods we fail to apply them because we don't practice very much. And when you don't do something a lot, you never get very good at it.

So too it could be that patients in our medical system think their doctors are rushed and don't care about them as individuals because, in fact, the system has become overtaxed and the pressure to see a volume of patients is too intense to allow doctors to linger with any one. But more simply it could be that doctors don't practice communicating effectively, efficiently, and humanely with patients, who thus report feeling rushed when all they want is to feel understood.

So too it could be, as the Heath brothers point out, that a thousand situations where the problem appears to be resistance to change are actually lack of clarity: "I don't know exactly what to do, and I don't know how to do it, *because I've never practiced it.*" To continue with the old-school philosophical theme, it is worth recalling the much quoted observation of Aristotle's that "we are what we repeatedly do," and that "excellence, then, is not an act, but a habit."

Practice, in this framework, is perhaps defined not as a series of drills and activities and scrimmages but as the opportunity to invent or reinvent ourselves in whatever way we wish, by repeatedly doing these activities with strategy and intentionality. We can become not just better surgeons and teachers and soccer players through practice, but better people. As Aristotle also observed, "We become just by performing just actions, temperate by performing temperate actions, brave by performing brave action." We wish, then, not only better skill and greater accomplishment for you, your organization, and your family but justice, temperance, bravery, and success, both in your practices and in the ten thousand games and performances that make up your life's work.

TEACHING TECHNIQUES FROM *TEACH LIKE A CHAMPION*

*T*hroughout this book, we make reference to the techniques in Doug's book, Teach Like a Champion, by describing activities we use to train teachers to use the techniques effectively, and by describing their use in running practices. For ease of reference, eight of the techniques are summarized here.

TECHNIQUE: STRONG VOICE

Strong Voice is a technique that allows teachers (and coaches) to replicate the skill of teachers who can "command a room." These teachers can enter a loud and unruly venue, which others would struggle to bring order to, and instantly get people to do as they ask or engage people who aren't listening (or don't want to listen) and get them focused.

Strong Voice teachers use five principles to signal their authority.

Economy of Language.   Fewer words are usually stronger than more. Being chatty signals nervousness and indecision while choosing words carefully shows preparedness and clarity of purpose. Be careful to remove all extraneous words, especially when you are nervous. Use a simple sentence structure. Make one crisp, clear point at a time. This allows you to ensure that messages of primary importance are not diluted by messages of secondary importance. Watch to see that your directions are followed. When you need to be all business, be clear and crisp, and then stop talking.

Do Not Talk Over.   Make a habit of showing that your words matter by waiting until there is no other talking before you begin. By ensuring that your voice doesn't compete for attention, you demonstrate that the decision to listen isn't situational. To achieve this goal you will probably need to use a "self-interrupt"; that is, start a sentence and break it at some obvious and awkward point to show that you will not go on until you have full attention.

For example, a teacher planned to address his class with a direction: "Students, I need your binders out so you can write down the homework correctly." If listeners weren't attentive, he might cut off his own sentence, ideally at a noticeable place, and remain silent for a few seconds before starting again: "Students, I need your—" If the low-level muttering and distractions did not entirely disappear, he might initiate another self-interrupt, this time with a bit less of the direction given: "Students, I—" During these interruptions he might stand stock-still to demonstrate that nothing could continue until attentiveness was restored.

Do Not Engage.   Once you have set the topic of conversation, avoid engaging in other topics until you have satisfactorily resolved the topic you initiated. This is especially important when the topic is behavioral follow-through.

Suppose, for example, that David is pushing Margaret's chair with his foot. You say, "David, please take your foot off of Margaret's chair." David replies, "But she's pushing me!" or "But she keeps on moving into my space!" Many teachers might engage the distraction David has proposed by saying, "Margaret, were you doing that?" or even, "I'm not really concerned with what Margaret was doing." This, however, means responding to David's choice of topic, not making him engage yours. A better response would be to say, "David, I asked you to take your foot off of Margaret's chair," or even, "Right now I need you to follow my direction and take your foot off of Margaret's chair." These responses make explicit reference to the fact that you initiated a topic and expect it to be addressed.

Another possible reply from David in the above situation might be, "But I wasn't doing anything!" Again, the best strategy is not to engage his topic. After all, you wouldn't have corrected him if you'd had a question in your mind about whether David's foot was where it should be. The best reply is, "I asked you to take your foot off Margaret's chair." Once you've done that, you don't need to say anything more.

In a coaching setting, you might be giving directions when a participant asks about something else. "Is this going to be like the fast-break drill?!" Rather than saying, "Well, a little bit, but we're working on something else" or even "That's right," you might simply pause briefly, put your finger to your lips, and then continue what you were saying. If you engage the distraction when you are trying to give directions, however, you will encourage more of the same. You will find that you rarely give directions clearly or effectively.

Square Up/Stand Still. In every comment you make, you speak nonverbally as well as with words. Your body can show that you expect people to follow your request. When you want to express the seriousness of your directions, turn with two feet and two shoulders to face the object of your words directly. Make sure your eye contact is direct. Stand up straight or lean in close (this shows your level of control by demonstrating that you are not shy or afraid; you don't crouch down to a dog you fear will bite you). If the student to whom you are speaking is distant, move towards him.

When giving directions that you want followed, stop moving and don't engage in other tasks at the same time. If you are passing out papers while you direct students, you suggest that your directions aren't that important. After all, you're doing other things at the same time too. At times it may even help to strike a formal pose, putting your arms behind your back, to show that you take your own words seriously and that they, like you, are formal and purposeful.

Quiet Power. When you get nervous, when you are worried that students might not follow your directions, when you sense that your control may be slipping away, your first instinct is often to talk louder and faster. When you get loud and talk fast, you *show* that you are nervous, scared, out of control. You send a message to students that if they can control you and your emotions, then they can make you put on a show that's much more entertaining than revising a paper or nailing coordinate geometry, say. When you get loud, you also, ironically, make the room louder and thus make it easier for students to successfully talk under their breath. Though it runs against all your instincts, get slower and quieter when you want control. Drop your voice. Make students strain to listen. Exude poise and calm.

TECHNIQUE: 100%

There is one acceptable percentage of students following a direction given in your classroom: 100%. This may sound draconian, but it is achieved primarily with finesse; in the classrooms of champion teachers the culture of compliance is both positive and—most important—invisible. Great teachers achieve 100% compliance through the effective application of three principles.

1. Use the least invasive form of intervention.

The goal is to get 100% compliance *so you can teach.* Getting compliance via constant, time-consuming disruptions causes the "death spiral." In breaking the concentration of students who were attentive, the interruptions get *everyone* off task. The solution is to correct without stopping or while stopping as briefly as possible and with as little distraction from the content of your lesson. Here are six forms of intervention, in order of invasiveness. Try to use the first ones as much as you can:

a. *Nonverbal correction:* Gesture to or establish eye contact with off-task students *while doing something else, preferably teaching the others.* As an example, you might gesture to a student asking him to put his hand down while you are talking.

b. *Positive group correction:* Make a quick verbal reminder *to the group* about what students *should be doing* (not what they shouldn't be doing). For example: "We're following along in our books"; "You should be tracking the speaker." Use this just as student attention appears on the brink of wandering. Earlier is better.

c. *Anonymous individual correction:* Make a quick verbal reminder to the group, similar to positive group correction above except that the anonymous individual correction makes it explicit that not everyone is where he or she needs to be.

   Examples: "We need two people." "Fifth grade, please check yourselves to make sure you've got your eyes on the speaker."

d. *Private individual correction:* When and if you have to name names, correct privately and quietly. Walk by the off-task student's desk. Lean down and, using a voice that preserves as much privacy as possible, tell the student quickly and calmly what to do. Then talk about something else.

   Example: "Quentin, I've asked everyone to track me, and I need to see you doing it too."

e. *Lightning-quick public correction:* Private correction is not always possible. Your goals in making a public correction should be (1) to limit the amount of time a student is "on stage" for something negative, and (2) to focus on telling the student what to do right rather than scolding or explicating what he did wrong.

Example: "Quentin, I need your eyes. Looking sharp, back row!"

f. *Consequence:* If a situation cannot be addressed quickly and successfully without a consequence, the consequence must be given so that instruction is not interrupted. As with other interventions, consequences should be delivered quickly and in the least invasive, least emotional manner. Ideally, a teacher has a scaled series of consequences from which to choose so that she can both match the significance of the response to the disruption and ensure her own ability to administer it quickly, decisively, and without wavering.

2. Rely on firm, calm finesse.

- *Catch it early:* Champion teachers catch off-task behavior early, as eyes begin to wander and before they've locked in on and begun to engage a distraction, for example.
- *"Thank you" is the strongest phrase:* Saying "thank you" after a student has done what you asked not only underscores civility but emphasizes for the rest of the class that the student in question did what you asked. (Why else would you thank the student?) This normalizes compliance and makes you seem calm, civil, and in control.
- *Purpose, not power:* Achieving compliance is an exercise in purpose, not power. Students need to follow directions so that they can be assured of having the best chance to succeed.

Responsiveness is the means, not the end. "I need your eyes on me so you can learn" is a more effective statement than "I asked for your eyes on me. When I ask you to do something, I expect you to do it."

- *Universal language:* Champion 100% teachers stress the universality of expectations. Their language reinforces this: "I need everyone sitting up," or even better, "We need everyone sitting up," which stresses universality better than "I need your eyes, Trevor."

3. Emphasize compliance you can see.

- *Invent ways to maximize visibility:* Find ways to make it easier to see who's followed your directions by asking students to do things that you can see. Asking for eyes on you is better than asking for attention because you can see it when you have it; and asking for pencils down *and* eyes on you is better yet since it gives you two things you can see, and because the second thing you've asked for—pencils down—is far easier to see in a quick scan of the room than is eye contact.
- *Be seen looking:* When you ask for compliance, make sure to look for it and to be seen looking for it. Every few minutes you should scan the room with a calm smile on your face to ensure that everything is as it should be. When you give a direction, remember to pause and scan the room. Narrating your scan— "Thank you, Peter. Thank you, Marissa. Eyes right on me, front row"—reinforces that when you ask for something, you then look to see who's done it and you consistently observe what individuals do. You show that you have "radar."
- *Avoid marginal compliance:* It's not just whether your students do what you've asked but whether they do it right. A certain number will complete a task only as fully as you show them what you expect. They'll rightly want to know what exactly "Eyes on me" means. Eyes near you? Eyes on yours for a fleeting second?

Eyes locked on yours while you're talking? The difference between these three interpretations is night and day.

TECHNIQUE: COLD CALL

To Cold Call is to call on students regardless of whether they have raised their hand. You ask a question and then you call the name of the student you want to answer it. When students see you frequently and reliably calling on students who don't have their hand raised, they come to expect it and prepare for it. Calling on whomever you choose regardless of whether a hand is up brings several critical benefits to your classroom.

First, Cold Call allows you to check for understanding far more effectively and systematically. It's critical to be able to check what any student's level of mastery is at any time, *regardless of whether he or she is offering to tell you.* In fact it's most important when he or she is *not* offering to tell you. Cold Call allows you to check on exactly the student(s) you want to check on to assess varying levels of mastery. When students are used to being asked by their teacher to participate or answer, they react to it as a normal event; this allows you to get a focused, honest answer and therefore check reliably for understanding. Of course this means that you'll also do best if you use the technique *before* you need to check for understanding. Your goal should be to normalize it as a natural and upbeat part of your class.

Second, Cold Call increases speed, in terms of your pacing and in terms of the rate at which you can cover material; both are critical issues. To understand the degree to which this is so, make an audiotape of your lesson sometime. Use a stopwatch to track how much time you spend waiting (and encouraging and cajoling and asking) for volunteers. With Cold Call you no longer have the delay after you ask, "Can anyone tell me what one cause of World War One was?" You no longer have to scan the room and wait for hands. You no longer have to dangle hints to encourage participants or tell your students that you'd like to see more hands. Instead of saying, "I'm seeing the same four hands. I want to hear from more of you. Doesn't anyone else know this?" you simply say, "Tell us one cause of World War One please, [slight pause here] Darren." Using Cold Call, you'll find you move through material much faster, and the tedious, momentum-sapping mood when no one appears to want to speak up will disappear. These two results will increase your pacing—the illusion of speed you create in your classroom—which is a critical factor in how students engage.

Third, Cold Call allows you to distribute work more broadly around the room and signal to students not only that they are likely to be called on to participate, and therefore that they should engage in the work of the classroom, but that you *want* to know what they have to say. You care about their opinion. Many students have insight to add to your class but are simply not the kind to offer unless pushed or asked. They may wonder if anyone really cares what they think. Or they think it's just as easy to keep their thoughts to themselves because Charlie's hand is always up anyway. Or they have a risky and potentially valuable thought on the tip of their tongue but aren't quite sure enough to say it aloud yet. Sometimes there will even be a glance, a moment when this student looks at you as if to say, "Should I?" or maybe even, "Just call on me and you'll share responsibility if this is totally off the mark." Many people mistakenly perceive Cold Call to be chastening, stressful. When you've watched tape of champion teachers Cold Calling, you'll know that it's not. In fact, when it's done well, it's an extremely powerful *and positive* way to reach out to kids and say, "I want to hear what you say"—even if Charlie's hand is up for the tenth time in twelve questions.

The success of the technique relies on the application of a few key principles:

• Cold Call should be predictable. The behavior you want (attentiveness) comes *before* you call on students, so the more predictable it is—students know it is likely to happen—the more effective it will be. Cold Call frequently and regularly. It's fine to let students know it's coming.

- Cold Calling should be systematic; that is, it should apply to everyone regardless of behavior or other factors. Call on multiple students. Distribute Cold Calls around the room, and eschew language that makes it seem like they happen because of something a student did or said.
- Keep Cold Calls positive. Make sure a Cold Call isn't a "gotcha" but an invitation to a real question. And make sure your goal is for students to get it right.
- Unbundle your Cold Calls by breaking up large questions into smaller ones and distributing them around the room. Why ask one question of one student—"What do you think was the most important cause of the Civil War, and why? David?"— when you could ask more than half a dozen questions of multiple students: "How many major causes of the Civil War does the author discuss—David? And what was one of them— Tyron? And another—Sarah? And the last—Jason? And which one do you think was most important—Carson? Do you agree—Mirela? Why?"

TECHNIQUE: RIGHT IS RIGHT

When responding to answers in class, the job of the teacher is to set a high standard for correctness, to hold out for 100%. There's a strong likelihood that students will stop striving when they hear the word "right" (or "yes" or some other proxy), so you should only name as "right" that which is truly and completely right. Students must not be betrayed into thinking they can do something that they cannot.

Many teachers respond to an almost correct answer a student may give in class by "rounding up." That is, they'll affirm the student's answer and add some detail of their own to make it fully correct, even though the student didn't provide it and may not recognize the differentiating factor as being significant. Imagine a student who is asked at the beginning of *Romeo and Juliet* how the Capulets and Montagues get along. "They don't like each other," the student might say, in an answer that most teachers would, I hope, want some elaboration upon before they called it fully correct. "Right," the teacher might say, "they don't like each other and they have been feuding for generations." That's the round-up. Sometimes the teacher will even give students credit for the round-up as if they said what they did not and what she, in fact, merely wished they'd said: "Right, what Kiley said was that they don't like each other and have been feuding. Good work, Kiley." In either case, the teacher has set a low standard for correctness in her class.

When answers are three-quarters correct, it's important to tell students that they're almost there, that you like what they've done so far, that they're closing in on the right answer, that they've done some good work or made a great start. You can repeat a student's answer back to him so he can listen for what's missing and further correct ("You said the Capulets and the Montagues didn't get along . . ."). Or you can wait, prod, encourage, cajole, or in other ways tell a student what still needs doing, or ask who can help get the class all the way there ("Kiley, you said the Capulets and the Montagues 'didn't get along.' Does that really capture their relationship? Does that sound like what they'd say about each other?"), until you get students *all the way to a version of being right that's rigorous enough to be college prep.*

Though as teachers we are the defenders of right answers, of the standards of correctness, there are in fact four ways in which we are at risk of slipping in holding out for "right." These lead us to the four categories within the Right Is Right technique.

Hold Out for All the Way.   Great teachers praise students for their effort but never confuse effort with mastery. A right answer includes the negative sign if a negative sign is warranted. There is no such thing as "Right! Except you need a negative sign." When you ask for the definition of a noun and get "a person, place or thing," don't do students the disservice of overlooking the fact that the answer is incomplete (a noun is a person, place, thing, or idea).

Answer My Question.   As a student you learn quickly in school that when you don't know the right answer to a question, you can usually get by if you answer a different one or if you say something true and heartfelt about the wider world. Can't identify the setting in the story? Offer an observation about the theme of injustice in the novel. "This reminds me of something from my neighborhood . . ." Most teachers can't pass up a student's taking on issues of justice and fairness, even if what they asked about was the setting. Over time, students come to recognize this.

If you're a Right Is Right teacher, though, you know that the "right" answer to any question other than the one you asked is wrong. You should insist that the student answer the question you asked, not the one she wished you asked or what she confused it for. You can respond with something like, "We'll talk about that in a few minutes, Daniella. Right now I want to know about the setting."

Another situation in which students answer a different question than the one you asked is when they conflate two pieces of information about a topic. You ask for a definition and they give you an example. You ask them to describe a concept and they provide the formula to solve it. If you start to listen for them, you'll find these sequences are far more common than you'd expect.

If you ask your students for a definition and get an example, say, "James, that's an example. I want the definition." After all, knowing the difference between an example and a definition matters.

Right Answer, Right Time.   Accepting a student's answer before all the steps required to get there have been shown deprives the rest of the students a full understanding of the process. It's tempting to think that it's a good thing the class is moving ahead quickly, but it's not. Teaching a repeatable process is more important than teaching the answer to a problem. It cheats the class if you respond favorably to one student's desire to move ahead to the end.

Say: "My question wasn't about the solution to the problem. It was about what we do next. What *do* we do next?"

Similarly, if you are asking the class what motivates a character's actions at the beginning of a chapter, you should resist accepting or engaging with an answer that discusses—even insightfully—the more dramatic events that conclude the chapter, especially if the point of discussing the first part is to better understand the ending (when you get there). You should protect the integrity of your lesson by not jumping ahead to engage an exciting "right" answer at the wrong time.

Use Technical Vocabulary. Good teachers get students to develop effective right answers using terms they are already comfortable with ("Volume is the amount of space something takes up"); *great* teachers get them to use precise technical vocabulary ("Volume is the amount of space an object occupies"). This expands student vocabularies and builds comfort with the terms students will need when they compete in college.

TECHNIQUE: WHAT TO DO

Champion teachers recognize that some portion of student noncompliance—a larger portion than many teachers ever suppose—is caused by students misunderstanding a direction, not knowing how to follow it, or tuning out in a moment of benign distraction. Recognizing this means giving directions to your students in a way that provides clear and useful guidance, enough of it to allow any student who *wanted* to do as asked to do so easily. The name for this technique is What to Do, and using it makes directions routinely useful and easy to follow.

What to Do starts, logically, with your telling students what to do—that is, not with telling them what *not* to do. We spend a lot of

time defining the behavior we want by its negative: "Don't get distracted." "Stop fooling around." "Cut it out." "That behavior was
inappropriate." These commands are vague, inefficient, and unclear.
They force students to guess what you want them to do. What's the "it"
in "Cut it out," for example? Assuming George doesn't want to get
distracted, if all you tell him is not to do something, what should
George assume the alternative is, and how would he know it?

Even when we don't define behavior by its negative, we
are often insufficiently helpful. When you tell a student to "pay
attention," ask yourself: Does she *know* how to pay attention?
Has anyone ever taught her? Does she know my specific expectations for paying attention (having her eyes on the speaker, say)?
Has anyone ever helped her learn to avoid and control distractions and distractedness? The command "pay attention" provides
no useful guidance. It fails to teach.

As teachers, one of our primary jobs is to tell students what to do
and how to do it. Telling students what to do rather than what *not* to
do is far more efficient and effective, and it refocuses us—even in
moments that are about behavior—on teaching. It expresses the
belief that teaching can solve problems. However, just telling
kids "what to do" is not quite enough. To really be effective,
directions should be specific, concrete, sequential, and observable.

- *Specific:* Effective directions are specific. They focus on manageable and precisely described actions that students can take.
  Instead of advising a student to pay attention, for example,
  I might advise him to put his pencil on his desk. Or keep his eyes
  on me. This provides useful guidance that a student can take
  action on and pay attention to. It is easy to remember. It is
  solution oriented. And it is very hard to misunderstand.
- *Concrete:* Effective directions are not just specific but involve clear,
  actionable tasks that any student knows how to do. If I tell my
  student to pay attention, he may or may not know how to do that,
  but if I tell him to put his feet under his desk, I have asked him to

do something no student can misunderstand or not know how to do. If he appears to struggle, I can get more concrete: "Turn your body to face me. Bring your legs around. Put them under your desk. Push in your chair." These are real things: physical, simple, commonplace. There is no gray area in this command and no finesse or prior knowledge required to follow through. As I will discuss in a moment, the elimination of such gray areas allows me to better understand the intention of my student.

- *Sequential:* Since a complex skill like paying attention is rarely a single, specific action, effective directions should describe a sequence of concrete, specific actions. In the case of my student who needs help paying attention, I might advise him, "John, put your feet under your desk, put your pencil down, and put your eyes on me." If John's a little further along, I might add, "When I write it on the board, that means you write it in your notes."

- *Observable:* In John's case, I was careful to give him not just any sequence of specific steps to follow; I described *observable actions*. I asked him to do things that I could plainly see him do. This is critical. The observational component of my directions left John with very little wiggle room in terms of his accountability. If I just tell him to "pay attention," I can't really observe whether he has done so and therefore I cannot hold him accountable very effectively. He will say, "But I *was* paying attention." Consciously or unconsciously, students sense and exploit this lack of accountability. However, if I tell John, "Put your feet under your desk, put your pencil down, and get your eyes on me," I can see perfectly well whether he has done it. *He* knows perfectly well that I can see whether he has done it. He is therefore more likely to do it.

TECHNIQUE: NO OPT OUT

A sequence that begins with a student unable or unwilling to answer a question should end whenever possible with that student giving the right answer. There can be two causes of the student's initial failure: he or she can be earnestly trying but lack the knowledge or skill to answer, or the student can essentially be refusing to try, using "I don't know" as a tool to get the teacher to leave him alone for the rest of the lesson, the rest of the day, or the rest of the year.

Either way, you want the student to be successful. Students need to rehearse success, and you need an approach that establishes accountability for effort. With No Opt Out, if they don't try, they save no effort because they'll still have to answer in the end.

There are four basic formats of No Opt Out:

Format 1: You provide the answer; your student repeats the answer.

TEACHER: What's the subject, James?

STUDENT 1: *Happy.*

TEACHER: James, when I ask you for the subject, I am asking for who or what the sentence is about. This sentence is about *mother*, James. That means *mother* is the subject. Now you tell me. What's the subject?

STUDENT 1: The subject is *mother.*

TEACHER: Good, James. The subject is *mother.*

Format 2: Another student provides the answer; the initial student repeats the answer.

TEACHER: What's the subject, James?

STUDENT 1: *Happy.*

TEACHER: Who can tell James what I am asking for when I ask for the subject?

STUDENT 2: You're asking for who or what the sentence is about.

TEACHER: Yes, I am asking for who or what the sentence is about. Peter, who or what is this sentence about?

STUDENT 2: *Mother.*

TEACHER: Good. Now you, James. What's the subject?

STUDENT 1: The subject is *mother.*

TEACHER: Yes, the subject is *mother.*

Format 3: You provide a cue; your student uses it to find the answer.

TEACHER: What's the subject, James?

STUDENT 1: *Happy.*

TEACHER: James, when I ask you for the subject, I am asking for who or what the sentence is about. Now, James, what's the subject?

STUDENT 1: *Mother.*

TEACHER: Good, James. The subject is *mother.*

Format 4: Another student provides a cue; the initial student uses it to find the answer.

TEACHER: What's the subject, James?

STUDENT 1: *Happy.*

TEACHER: Who can tell James what I am asking for when I ask for the subject?

STUDENT 2: You're asking for who or what the sentence is about.

TEACHER: Yes, I am asking for who or what the sentence is about. James, what's the subject?

STUDENT 1: *Mother.*

TEACHER: Good, James. The subject is *mother.*

TECHNIQUE: POSITIVE FRAMING

People are motivated by the positive far more than the negative. Seeking success and happiness will spur stronger action than seeking to avoid punishment. Psychological studies repeatedly show that people are far more likely to be spurred to action by a vision of a positive outcome than they are by avoiding a negative one. So while you should still fix and improve behavior relentlessly, strive to do so as positively as you can, using these six rules:

Live in the Now.   In public, that is, in front of your class or while your lesson is underway, avoid harping on what students can no longer fix. Focus corrective interactions on the things students should do *right now* to succeed from this point forward. There's a time and place for processing what went wrong; avoid making that time when your lesson hangs in the balance, and avoid making that place in front of class. Give instructions describing what the next move on the path to success is. Say, "Keana, I need your eyes forward," not "Keana, stop looking back at Tanya."

Assume the Best.   Don't attribute to ill intention what could be the result of distraction, lack of practice, or genuine misunderstanding. Until you know an action was intentional, your public discussion of it should remain positive, showing that you assume your students have tried (and will try) to do as you've asked. Saying, "Just a minute, class, some people don't seem to think they have to push in their chairs when we line up," assumes selfishness, deliberate disrespect, and laziness. Not only is it more positive to say, "Just a minute, class, some people seem to have forgotten to push in their chairs," but it shows your faith and trust in your students.

Further, assuming the worst makes you appear weak. Showing that you assume your students are always trying to comply with your wishes suggests that you assume everyone knows you're in charge. By contrast, saying, "If you can't sit up, Charles, I'll have to keep you in from recess," reveals your suspicion that Charles will disobey you. Say, "Show me your best, Charles," and walk away (for the moment) as if you couldn't imagine a world in which he wouldn't do it.

Allow Plausible Anonymity.   Allow students the opportunity to strive towards your expectations in anonymity *as long as they are making a good-faith effort.* Begin by correcting them without using their names, when possible. If a few students struggle to follow your directions, consider making your first correction something like, "Check yourself to make sure you've done exactly what I've asked." In most cases this will yield results faster than calling out laggards. Saying to your class, "Wait a minute, Homeroom Harvard [or "Tigers" or "fifth grade" or just "guys"], I hear calling out. I need to see you quiet and ready to go!" is better than lecturing the callers-out in front of the class. And as with "assume the best" (earlier), you can still administer consequences while preserving anonymity: "Some people didn't manage to follow directions the whole way, so let's try that again." When there is no good-faith effort by students, it may no longer be plausible to maintain anonymity, but "naming names" shouldn't be your first move. Remember that you can deliver consequences anonymously and that doing so stresses shared responsibility among your students. Some students weren't doing their job and we all own the consequence.

Build Momentum/Narrate the Positive. Compare the statements two teachers recently made in their respective classrooms:

TEACHER 1:   [*Stopping before giving a direction*] I need three people. Make sure you fix it if that's you! Now I need two. We're almost there. Ah, thank you. Let's get started. . . .

TEACHER 2:   [*Same setting*] I need three people. And one more student doesn't seem to understand the directions, so now I need four. Some people don't appear to be listening. I am waiting, gentlemen. If I have to give detentions, I will.

In the first teacher's classroom, things appear to be moving in the right direction because the teacher narrates the evidence of his own command, of students doing as they're asked, of things getting better. *He calls his students' attention to this fact, and this normalizes it.* Students are arguably more accountable for their behavior in the first room, but nobody seems to notice because failure seems so unlikely.

The second teacher is telling a story that no one wants to hear: from the outset students can smell the fear, the weakness, and the inevitable unhappy ending. Everything is wrong and getting worse, generally without consequence. Students can hardly fear accountability when their teacher is describing their peers' impunity ("Some people don't appear to be listening").

Great teachers conjure momentum by normalizing the positive. They draw attention to the good and the "getting better." Narrating your weakness only makes your weakness seem normal. If you say, "Some students didn't do what I asked," you have made that situation public. Now your choice is consequence or countenance.

Challenge!   Kids love to be challenged. They love to prove they can do things. They love to compete. They love to win. So challenge them; exhort them to prove what they can do; build competition into the day. Some examples:

"You guys have been doing a great job this week. Let's see if you
    can take it up a notch."
"I love the tracking I see. I wonder what happens when I move
    back here."
"Let's see if we can get these papers out in 12 seconds. Ready?!"
"Good is not good enough. I want to see perfect today!"
"Ms. Austin said she didn't think you guys could knock out your
    math tables louder than her class. And they're sitting across the
    hall right now. Let's show 'em what we've got!"
"Let's see which row has got this information down! We'll use a
    little friendly wager: the row where everyone gets it correct the
    fastest can skip the first two problems on the homework set!"

Talk Expectations and Aspiration.   Talk about who your students are becoming and where they're going. Frame praise in those terms. When your class looks great, tell them they look "college," tell them they look like "scholars," tell them you feel like you're sitting in the room with future presidents and doctors and artists. While it's nice that you're proud of them and while it's certainly wonderful to tell them that, in the end the goal is not for them to please you but to leave you behind on a long journey towards a more important goal than making you happy. It's useful then if your praise sets a goal larger than your own opinion. On a more micro level, seek opportunities that reaffirm expectations around smaller details. When you're correcting, say, "In this class we always track," not "Some people aren't giving us their best attention." Finish an activity by saying, "If you finish early, check your work. Make sure you get 100% today." Keep their eyes on the prize by constantly referring to it with your words.

TECHNIQUE: FORMAT MATTERS

It's not just what students say that matters but how they communicate it. To succeed, students must take their knowledge and express it in a variety of clear and effective formats to fit the demands of the situation, and of society. The complete sentence is the battering ram that knocks down the door to college. The essays required to enter college (and every paper written once there) demand absolute fluency with syntax. Conversations with potential employers require subject–verb agreement. In the working world, spelling counts. To prepare students to succeed in that world, master teachers do students the favor of requiring complete sentences, correct spelling, and proficient grammar in their classrooms and reinforcing it *every chance they get*. It's not enough to have great ideas; students have to present great ideas in the format that makes them valuable, in the language of opportunity.

Champion teachers rely on a few basic format expectations:

- *Grammatical format:* Great teachers correct syntax, usage, and grammar in the classroom even if they believe the divergence from "standard" is acceptable or normal in other settings.

Two simple methods that involve no discussion and no judgment beyond identification of the error itself are especially helpful:

○ *Identify the error:* When a student makes a grammatical error, merely repeat the error in an interrogative tone:
"We *was* walking down the street?"
"There *gots to be* eight of them?"

Then allow the student to self-correct. If the student fails to self-correct, use the "begin the correction" technique (below) or quickly provide the correct syntax and ask him or her to repeat. This builds familiarity with the language of opportunity and ensures that there's no incentive to pretend not to know the answer—you're still going to have to repeat it anyway.

○ *Begin the correction:* When a student makes a grammatical error, the teacher *begins* to rephrase the answer as it would sound if grammatically correct and allows the student to complete it. In the examples above, that would mean saying "We *were* . . ." or "There *has* to . . ." and expecting the student to provide the full correct answer.

• *Complete sentence format:* Insist upon answers being delivered in complete sentences; strive to give students the maximum amount of practice at this critical skill. Use several methods to support students in practicing using complete sentences over and over in speaking and writing. For example, you can

○ Provide the first words of a complete sentence to show students how to begin sentences. This is especially important when students are not yet ready to answer every question on their own in a complete sentence, as in this exchange:
TEACHER: James, how many tickets are there?
JAMES: Six.
TEACHER: There are . . .
JAMES: There are six tickets in the basket.

○ Remind students before they start to answer. End your questions by "punctuating" them with the letters "RTQ," short for "repeat the question." Do this after every question as students are learning this skill, as in

TEACHER: Jamal, what's the setting of the story? RTQ.
STUDENT: The setting is the city of Los Angeles in the
    year 2013.

○ Remind students afterwards with a quick and simple reminder with the lowest possible transaction cost, as in

TEACHER: What was the year of Caesar's birth?
STUDENT: 100 BC.
TEACHER: Like a scholar, please.
STUDENT: Julius Caesar was born in 100 BC.

• *Audible format:* Insist that answers are delivered in a loud, clear voice. What's the point of discussing answers with 30 people if only a few can hear what you're talking about? If it matters enough to say in class, then it matters that everyone can hear it. If not, an unspoken but damning message about the importance of what happens in that room is delivered: class discussion and student participation are afterthoughts, take them or leave them. Underscore that students should be listening to their peers by insisting that their peers make themselves audible.

In short, when you're teaching, set expectations for quality that will ultimately be internalized and build the habits of mind that drive achievement. Know that the assessments that grant access to higher learning demand certain formats as well, so there's little sense in exempting students from the formats they'll have to master to get into college.

SAMPLE PRACTICE ACTIVITIES

Here we include three sample practice activities that we use when training teachers and school leaders on using and practicing the techniques from *Teach Like a Champion*. We hope that these practice activities will provide additional context for how they are discussed in the book as well as concrete examples of how the rules of practice are applied in discrete practice activities.

NO OPT OUT ITERATIVE PRACTICE

Background. Champion teachers are quick to establish the expectation that even when students don't know an answer (yet!), they still have the responsibility to participate in the learning process. One of the ways to accomplish this is through No Opt Out, a technique that ensures that a student who is unable to answer a question will answer it as often as possible.

    Objective of the Practice. Our objective with this activity was to get teachers to use No Opt Out immediately after it had been introduced. In order to do that, we simplified the activity in order to

(1) give participants enough iterations so that they started to feel natural with it (Rule 3: Let the Mind Follow the Body), and (2) have them practice simplified versions of different situations they might face so that they weren't worried about what could go wrong (Rule 10: Isolate the Skill). In short, we wanted them to practice being successful (Rule 1: Encode Success).

Task.   In this practice session there are three roles: Teacher, Student A, and Student Z. The Teacher will pose a question to Student A, who will not respond with the correct answer. The Teacher will use No Opt Out to enable Student A to respond with the correct answer. Your goal is to practice getting comfortable using No Opt Out in relatively simple and predictable settings. Listen for how your tone and body language change, so you can find the versions of each that are natural to you.

No Opt Out Iterative Practice
(Facilitator Directions)

Step 1 (5 minutes): Allow teachers to read through the four different variations on the Teacher Copy and plan how they would respond in each scenario.

Step 2 (2 minutes): Ask teachers to get into groups of three with three rotating roles:

1. Teacher
2. Student A
3. Student Z

Step 3 (20 minutes; 5 minutes per round): For each round, the basic exchange will remain consistent:

- The Teacher asks Student A a simple question: "What's 3 plus 5?"
- Student A is unable to answer, but in a different way (and with a different tone) each time, as indicated by each variation.

Teacher asks Student Z to provide a correct answer, then uses No Opt Out to return to Student A.

Once all teachers have completed the round, reflect briefly on the reflection question before the group moves on to the following variation. The purpose of this practice is not to practice using feedback but rather for teachers to get comfortable using the No Opt Out technique in a variety of realistic situations.

No Opt Out Iterative Practice
(Teacher Copy)

Variation 1: Student A should get the answer wrong but in a tone suggesting genuine effort. Student Z should answer directly and correctly. *Plan how you would respond.*

Reflection: Were you and your partners able to normalize error, that is, make Student A feel like getting the question wrong and then getting it right was a normal part of school? If so, what helped?

Variation 2: Student A should say "I don't know" in a sarcastic tone. Student Z should answer the question directly and correctly. *Plan how you would respond.*

Reflection: How did your response change when Student A was negative, challenging, and sarcastic? What were the two most effective things that members of the group did?

Variation 3: Student A should again answer incorrectly but in a tone suggesting genuine effort. Student Z should say "I don't know" when asked the follow-up question. *Plan how you would respond.*

Reflection: What actions or phrases were effective in this situation?

Variation 4: The fourth and final time through the exercise, Student A should get the answer wrong but in a tone suggesting genuine effort. Student Z should answer directly and correctly.

The Teacher should be ready with a more demanding question to push for greater rigor. *Plan how you would respond.*

Reflection: What actions or phrases were effective in this situation?

STRONG VOICE LAY-UP DRILL

Background.   Strong Voice (Economy of Language, Do Not Talk Over, Do Not Engage, Square Up/Stand Still, and Quiet Power) can have a powerful impact on students, often diffusing potentially explosive situations before they escalate beyond control. There are several reasons this activity is so powerful in practicing elements of Strong Voice:

- It allows all staff members/participants to play all roles and is a great way to create norms around role-playing because no one person is "on stage" (Rule 34: Everybody Does It).
- It normalizes the feedback process and challenges participants to provide honest feedback (Rule 23: Practice *Using* Feedback).
- It makes subtechniques more concrete by using these terms in feedback (Rule 40: Keep Talking).

Objective of the Practice.   Our objective with this activity was to give teachers repeated practice using the Strong Voice technique in the classroom. When using this activity, we usually choose three to four of the variations and eventually end with the final variation when we stop giving and getting feedback. At this point, the technique is becoming automatic to teachers, built into muscle memory (Rule 3: Let the Mind Follow the Body).

Task.   Participants will do a role play to practice using the Strong Voice technique in a common teacher–student interaction: asking a student who is slouching to sit up.

Strong Voice Lay-Up Drill
(Facilitator Directions)

Step 1 (5 minutes): Participants complete the table on the Lay-Up Drill by planning the Dos and Don'ts of implementing Strong Voice with students.

Step 2 (10 minutes): Participants line up according to the diagram at the bottom of the Strong Voice Lay-Up Drill.

Variation 1.0:

Directions:

- Each participant will rotate through the role play playing the Student, then becoming the Teacher, then becoming the Coach, who gives feedback, and then going to the back of the line to be the Student again.

Roles:

- *Student:* Slouch in your seat. Immediately comply with the Teacher's request to sit up.
- *Teacher:* Use the principles of Strong Voice to get the Student to sit up. For Variation 1.0, simply state "I need you to sit up." Do not vary the language.
- *Coach:* When providing feedback, include one thing that the Teacher did well and one thing that the Teacher could try differently. You may encourage the Coach to always use the following sentence starters:
  - "You did a good job of . . . "
  - "Next time, try . . . "

For example: "You did a good job of squaring up with the student. Next time, try to implement a nonverbal signal to support your direction."

Step 3 (20 minutes): Continue the Strong Voice drill, choosing several of the next different variations (3–5 minutes per variation).

Variations:

1. *Delayed Reaction:* Have the Student count to three in his/her head before complying with the Teacher's directions.
2. *Nonverbal:* Use only nonverbal signals (for example, a hand gesture) in order to get the Student to sit up.
3. *Immediate Feedback:* Immediately implement the feedback: The Teacher takes two turns in a row before becoming the Student, implementing the feedback immediately before getting in line.
4. *Best Kid on a Bad Day:* The Teacher responds to the Student as though it is one of his/her star students having a tough day.
5. *Economy of Language:* The Teacher may change the language he/she uses to ask the Student to sit up.
6. *No Feedback:* Do not give feedback (that is, drop the Coach role); cycle through the roles quickly in order to get in as many practice opportunities as possible.

Strong Voice Lay-Up Drill
(Teacher Copy)

You will be role-playing a scenario in which you ask a student to sit up. The purpose of this practice activity is to get as many opportunities as possible to practice using your Strong Voice. In the following table, list the Dos and Don'ts of using Strong Voice with students when delivering the direction "I need you to sit up."

Do	Don't

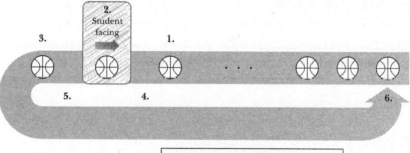

1. **Teacher** asks **Student** to sit up
2. **Student** complies
3. **Coach** behind **Student** provides feedback
4. **Teacher** becomes **Student**
5. **Student** becomes **Coach**
6. **Coach** moves to end of the line

USING NONVERBAL INTERVENTIONS
ROLE PLAY

Background. Nonverbal interventions are a critical part of "100%" classroom management. Done correctly, they can allow you to manage behavior while you continue teaching, keeping your lesson "on the rails." This allows you to avoid the "death spiral"—interrupting the learning for students who remain attentive—and to remain positive in dealing with those who are off task.

Objective of the Practice. The purpose of this activity is to give participants the opportunity to use and improve their use of nonverbal interventions to reinforce high behavioral expectations via the least invasive means, *while* teaching. We use a simple lesson here (teaching the Pledge of Allegiance) in order to *isolate the skill* of effectively using nonverbal interventions.

Task. Teachers will practice the effective use of nonverbal gestures (in the 100% technique) by participating in a role play in which they redirect off-task behavior nonverbally.

Using Nonverbal Interventions Role Play
(Facilitator Directions)

Step 1 (10 minutes): Ask participants to complete the Teacher Copy of the role play by describing a nonverbal intervention they could use to address each behavior if the behavior happened while they were teaching. Remind participants that the goal is to address behavior without stopping the lesson and that the best interventions are

- *Simple:* You want to use them fast
- *Unambiguous:* Reliability of interpretation is critical
- *Positive:* Call attention to the solution rather than the problem

You may wish to have all participants try the first example and then report back their answers before having them complete the rest of the worksheet.

Step 2 (5 minutes): Choose a few of the behaviors on the worksheet and ask participants to demonstrate a nonverbal intervention they might use. When possible, ask for several examples for each behavior (that is, from multiple participants) and ask participants to discuss the similarities and differences.

Step 3 (10 minutes):

Scenario: Announce that you will now offer participants the chance to put these and similar interventions into practice via a role play where a teacher will be required to correct behaviors while teaching. The objective for the lesson is to have the class learn and memorize the Pledge of Allegiance. Assign the following roles to participants:

Roles:

1. *Students:* Listen to the Teacher's lesson and comply with directions.
2. *"Confederates":* Two Students should take turns demonstrating the behaviors listed on the Teacher Copy, in order, approximately 15–20 seconds apart. Confederates should be spaced as far apart within the group as possible.
3. *Teacher:* Teach the Pledge of Allegiance to Students, using the nonverbal signals that have been planned in advance to redirect misbehavior.
4. *Coach:* Observe the role play and provide feedback to the Teacher on his/her use of nonverbal signals. You may use the following sentence starters:
   ○ "One thing you did well was . . . "
   ○ "One thing you can try differently next time is . . . "

The purpose is to force the Teachers to use effective gestures and nonverbal interventions while teaching. Thus, the Confederates should correct their behavior in a compliant manner if they feel that a simple, unambiguous, and relatively positive nonverbal intervention has been made.

Step 4 (5 minutes): Ask the teacher to repeat a small portion of the practice, integrating the feedback from his or her coach. After the initial teacher has practiced, you can switch roles, allowing for more teachers to practice.

Step 5 (10 minutes):

Discussion: Starting with the role-players, participants should be asked to reflect on the experience.

Questions for the "Teacher(s)":

- What was most difficult about the activity?
- What were your most effective interventions? Why?
- What helped you to manage the situation effectively?

Questions for the "Students":

- What did you notice about the teacher's interactions with you or your peers?
- As a student who was doing what was asked, did you feel engaged in, and important to, the lesson? Were you able to focus on it?

Step 6 (5 minutes): The previous activity revealed that there are more and less effective ways to intervene nonverbally. As a group make a list on the board of practical takeaways that are important to think about in making effective nonverbal interventions (for example, the importance of moving into a student's line of sight for a gesture).

Using Nonverbal Interventions Role Play
(Teacher Copy)

Listed here you'll find various types of student behavior that might require a nonverbal intervention. For each one, describe an effective nonverbal intervention you might use. The best interventions are

- *Simple:* You want to use them quickly while you are teaching
- *Unambiguous:* Reliability of interpretation is critical
- *Positive:* Call attention to the solution rather than the problem

The first example is done for you. Please continue with the behaviors and interventions that follow.

Behavior One: Student slouching in his chair
Intervention One: Make "hands folded" gesture (hands folded in front of me with elbows bent 90° and fingers intertwined) to signal to sit up.
Behavior Two: Student with her head down on her desk (eyes up)
Intervention Two:
Behavior Three: Student with her head down on her desk (eyes hidden)
Intervention Three:
Behavior Four: Student sending the bathroom signal at critical time during lesson
Intervention Four:

Behavior Five: Frequent struggler doing well and working hard today

Intervention Five:

Behavior Six: Student persistently raising hand (for reasons unrelated to your questions)

Intervention Six:

Behavior Seven: Student engaged in sustained looking under desk for "something"

Intervention Seven:

Behavior Eight: Student gazing out window

Intervention Eight:

NOTES

INTRODUCTION

1. We're not making this up. Wooden believed that haphazardly worn socks and poorly tied shoes were an epidemic that led to blisters, which in turn led to players—even players like Alcindor and Walton—missing games. So they started with socks.
2. This number excludes the portion of paid time at work—and therefore teacher salaries—spent in professional development.

RETHINKING PRACTICE

1. Thomas Rohlem and Gerald Le Tendre, *Teaching and Learning in Japan*, Cambridge University Press, 1998.

HOW TO PRACTICE

1. "In SEAL Team Six, Lessons from 'Horrible Night' in Iran 30 Years Ago." http://www.csmonitor.com/USA/Military/2011/0503/In-SEAL-Team-Six-success-lessons-from-horrible-night-in-Iran-30-years-ago
2. Michael Lewis, *Moneyball*, p. 148.
3. Michael Lewis, *Moneyball*, pp. 172−175.
4. Nearly everyone who has played soccer knows what this drill is from its name. Here is an example of using shared vocabulary for skills and drills.
5. http://performance.fourfourtwo.com/technique/improve-your-technique-with-manchester-united
6. http://www.washingtonpost.com/sports/redskins/when-it-comes-to-practice-the-redskins-pay-attention-to-every-detail/2011/12/22/gIQAEQqTCP_story_1.html

FEEDBACK

1. Eileen Lai Horng, Daniel Klasik, Susanna Loeb, *Principal Time Use and School Effectiveness*, Urban Institute, December 2009. http://www.urban.org/uploaded pdf/1001441-School-Effectiveness.pdf

CULTURE OF PRACTICE

1. http://www.ncbi.nlm.nih.gov/pmc/articles/PMC1002465/pdf /westjmed00107—0046.pdf
2. http://harvardmagazine.com/2012/03/twilight-of-the-lecture
3. *Moonwalking with Einstein*, p. 53.
4. http://www.newyorker.com/reporting/2011/10/03 /111003fa_fact_gawande
5. http://onpar.blogs.nytimes.com/2010/04/26/at-the-range-drive-less-and -practice-more/?scp=17&sq=practice&st=Search
6. http://onpar.blogs.nytimes.com/2010/04/26/at-the-range-drive-less-and -practice-more/?scp=17&sq=practice&st=Search
7. http://www.hec.fr/var/fre/storage/original/application/35794449631 be0c15c6a36e055ab10d2.pdf
8. Ronald Morrish, *Keys to Effective Discipline*, p. 148.
9. http://edreform.blogspot.com/2011_06_01_archive.html
10. *Teach Like a Champion*, p. 211.

POST-PRACTICE

1. U.S. Department of Education, National Center for Education Statistics, National Assessment of Educational Progress, "National Trends in Reading by Average Scale Scores." http://nces.ed.gov/nationsreportcard/pdf/main2008 /2009479.pdf
2. http://www.startinganedschool.org/2010/03/29/more-earbud/
3. http://www.webmd.com/anxiety-panic/guide/20061101/fear-public -speaking
4. *Teach Like a Champion*, p. 50.
5. http://online.wsj.com/article/SB10001424052702303678704576441823130334218.html?KEYWORDS=coach+K

6. http://online.wsj.com/article/SB100014240527023036787045764418231303
    34218.html?KEYWORDS=coach+K
7. Atul Gawande, *Better*, p. 187.

CONCLUSION

1. http://www.nytimes.com/2011/11/20/business/after-law-school-associates
    -learn-to-be-lawyers.html?pagewanted=all
2. http://www.nytimes.com/2011/11/20/business/after-law-school-associates
    -learn-to-be-lawyers.html?pagewanted=all
3. Larry Rohter, "The Actor as Architect of a Role," *New York Times*, December
    29, 2010.

ACKNOWLEDGMENTS

Our work together—and the ideas that ultimately became this book—began at Uncommon Schools, the incredible organization we are proud and honored to call home. The teachers and administrators in the schools Uncommon has founded are our heroes. Quietly and without a whiff of pomp or ceremony they get up—early!—every morning and strive to make the world a better place through diligence, passion, humility, and practice. So to our colleagues at Uncommon, and to the families who entrust us with your children's educations, thank you for letting us be a part of what you've built. Among those whose help and guidance on this book deserve specific mention, we gratefully acknowledge Norman Atkins, Evan Rudall, Brett Peiser, Josh Phillips, Rob Richard, Colleen Driggs, Hannah Solomon, Christy Lundy, John Costello, Tracey Koren, Julie Jackson, Sultana Noormuhammad, Miriam Cohen, Paul Bambrick, Laura Maestas, Paul Powell, David McBride, Kelli Ragin, Stacey Shells, Bill Sherman, and Katie's dedicated staff at Troy Prep, who have truly created a culture of practice.

We also owe a debt of gratitude to the larger sector of results-driven educators from great schools around the country, so many of whom have joined us at our "Train the Trainer" workshops.

You are too many to name, but thank you for all of the lessons you taught us as we stumbled forward—the rules in this book are yours as well.

Also a richly deserved thanks to our colleagues who engaged in reflection and discussion on the topic of "practice"—most of the good ideas come from "geeking out" with you. A special thanks to the many superstars who have provided thoughts and guidance in reading our drafts throughout this process. Among them, Heather Kirkpatrick, Matt Candler, Ben Marcovitz, Tim Daly, Dan Heath, Richard Cohen, Aaron Cohen, Asher Mendelsohn, Yoon Kang, and Dan Cotton, whom Katie will thank below for other reasons but from whose insight we all benefit, were incredibly generous with their time and incredibly helpful.

Our agent, Rafe Sagalyn, was as always sagacious and insightful. It's a gift to have someone you can trust completely with your life's work. At Jossey-Bass, we are extremely grateful for our tireless editor, Kate Gagnon, who guided us throughout our work. We are also indebted to Paula Stacey for her patient and tenacious editing, as well as Jeff Wyneken and Robin Lloyd and the entire team at Jossey-Bass headed by Lesley Iura.

Doug adds: Thank you, always, to Lisa. This is a book about engineering positive outcomes, but in marriage I know I'm plain lucky. And to Caden, Maia, and Willa, to whom I hope to give a dizzying dose of unlimited, unconditional love; the ability to shine at whatever sets their hearts on fire; and the diligence to get there through practice. Finally, to my mom, dad, and sister, all of whom are writers. How could I do anything else?

Katie adds: Thank you to my parents who believed in the power of practice and gave me a world of opportunities. David, Michael, and Sarah, thank you for modeling curiosity and determination. Aliza and Ezra, you have taught me so much as you grow and develop into thoughtful, loving, talented people. You have been patient and helpful as this book has come into being. To Dan, thank you for listening to drafts, trying out ideas and improving them, and being a wonderful, thoughtful dad to our two kids. I am incredibly lucky to have you as a colleague and partner in my work and my life. You inspire me to keep working at getting better.

Erica adds: Thank you to Mom and Dad for giving me countless opportunities to practice and learn. From encouraging me to play a musical instrument at a young age, to happily tolerating my love of horses and soccer, what I know about practice I first learned from you. To David and Laura, thank you for always being there for me as siblings, as models in life, and as friends. Thank you to my friends for all of your love and laughter. Thank you to the founding staff at Leadership Prep Bedford-Stuyvesant for starting this journey at Uncommon Schools with me. To Steve's family, thank you for your support. Most of all, thanks to my little family—my three boys, Charlie, George, and Steve: to Charlie and George for always reminding me of what is most important; and to Steve for supporting me every day in my work. Thank you mostly for practicing side by side with me in the most important job we will ever have: being parents to our kids.

A final thanks to all of the teachers and coaches whom we have each learned from over the years. Like you, we have spent our lives on the learning side of practice on our sports teams and ski and music lessons. We are thankful for your support, feedback, and for the opportunity to practice.

Doug Lemov's highly influential first book, *Teach Like a Champion*, was based on his study of top teachers in high-poverty public schools. He uses what he learned watching great teachers work their magic to train educators as part of his work at Uncommon Schools, the nonprofit school management organization he helped found. He holds a Bachelor of Arts from Hamilton College, a Master of Arts from Indiana University, and an MBA from the Harvard Business School. Visit Doug Lemov at www.douglemov.com and http://teachlikeachampion.wiley.com.

Erica Woolway is the chief academic officer for the *Teach Like a Champion* team at Uncommon Schools. In this role, she works with the team to train thousands of high-performing teachers and school leaders across the country each year—reaching over one million students. Prior to becoming CAO, she served as both dean of students and director of staff development at Uncommon Schools and as an adjunct literacy instructor at Relay Graduate School of Education. Erica began her career in education as a kindergarten teacher and then worked as a school counselor. She received her Bachelor of Arts in psychology and Spanish from

Duke University, a Master of Arts and Master of Education from Teachers College in school counseling, and her Master of Arts in school leadership from National Lewis University. She currently lives in New York City with her husband, their two boys, and their Chihuahua, Rita.

Katie Yezzi is the founding principal of True North Troy Preparatory Charter Elementary School, an Uncommon School in upstate New York. She taught for eight years in public middle and high schools in Northern and Southern California. She also served as English department head, schoolwide reform coordinator, and subsequently as assistant principal of curriculum and principal in district and charter high schools in San Francisco. She is a graduate of New Leaders, a nationally acclaimed program dedicated to training effective urban school principals. In 2008, she began working with Doug Lemov on teacher and instructional leader development related to *Teach Like a Champion*. Katie earned her Bachelor of Arts in American civilization and her Master of Arts in teaching English from Brown University. She lives in upstate New York with her husband and two children.

SUMMARY OF RULES

1. **Encode Success**
   Practice getting it right. Take the time to check for understanding and work for mastery before adding complexity. Remember, failure builds character better than it builds skills.

2. **Practice the 20**
   Be great at the things that matter most. Spend 80% of your time practicing the 20% of skills that are most important.

3. **Let the Mind Follow the Body**
   Get skills going on autopilot. Build up automated skills to master more complex situations.

4. **Unlock Creativity . . . with Repetition**
   You can't do higher level work if you are wasting brain power on the basics. Drill the fundamentals to free your mind to be creative when it matters most.

5. **Replace Your Purpose (with an Objective)**
   Purpose is not enough. Focus practice on measurable and manageable objectives.

6. **Practice "Bright Spots"**
   Tap into the power of what works. Find your strengths and use practice to make them stronger.

7. **Differentiate Drill from Scrimmage**
   To develop skills, use drills. Reserve scrimmage for evaluating performance readiness and mastery.

8. **Correct Instead of Critique**
   Help people repeat a task in a concretely different way rather than simply telling them what was wrong.

9. **Analyze the Game**
   The skills needed to deliver a winning performance are not always obvious. Watch, gather data, analyze, and let yourself be surprised.

10. **Isolate the Skill**
    New skills are best taught and practiced in isolation. Challenge yourself to define small, specific skills and to craft precise drills for each.

11. **Name It**
    Give skills a name and create a shared vocabulary for practice in order to focus people's discussion and reflection.

12. **Integrate the Skills**
    After initial mastery, weave together multiple skills in increasingly complex environments and situations.

13. **Make a Plan**
    Great practices depend on great planning. Create plans with data-driven objectives, detail activities down to the last minute, then rehearse and revise.

14. **Make Each Minute Matter**
    Every moment is precious. Find efficiencies and make them a routine part of practice.

15. **Model *and* Describe**

   Good teaching requires both showing *and* explaining to ensure understanding.

16. **Call Your Shots**

   When modeling—whether it may be a specific technique or how to run a meeting—alert observers to what you're trying to demonstrate so they see it happen. Help them watch strategically and with intention.

17. **Make Models Believable**

   Flawless modeling in ideal settings can be easy to dismiss. Ensure that modeling occurs in conditions that are true to life and credible.

18. **Try Supermodeling**

   Directly modeling a skill in context is an opportunity to show how other skills can be applied.

19. **Insist They "Walk *This* Way"**

   Many people resist imitating others, thinking it's cheating or uncreative. But sometimes this is the best way to learn. Make "copying" a good word and tell people what they should strive to copy.

20. **Model Skinny Parts**

   Break down complex skills into narrow steps, modeling each part separately. Let people succeed and then stop before they try to do more than they can successfully execute.

21. **Model the Path**

   Modeling the perfect result can sometimes lead to poor performance. Model the process of *how* to achieve as well as the achievement itself.

22. **Get Ready for Your Close-up**

   Video has many advantages. You can edit what gets shown, highlight important points, analyze, and review. Use it to capture real-life situations—both in the performance and in practice.

23. **Practice *Using* Feedback (Not Just Getting It)**

   It's one thing to accept feedback; it's another to actually use it. Make putting feedback into practice right away the expectation.

24. **Apply First, Then Reflect**

   Reflection is worthwhile, but it is best done after you've tried out feedback, not before.

25. **Shorten the Feedback Loop**

   Feedback works best when it's given (and used) immediately. Timing of feedback (and the right time is right away) beats strength of feedback every time.

26. **Use the Power of Positive**

   Feedback is not just a tool for repair. Identify what people do right, help them repeat it, and guide them to apply it in other settings.

27. **Limit Yourself**

   Too much feedback is overwhelming. Feedback from too many sources is confusing. Discipline yourself and others to keep feedback focused and productive.

28. **Make It an Everyday Thing**

   Make feedback the norm by consistently giving and receiving it from the start. Create an environment where feedback is not only accepted but welcomed.

29. **Describe the Solution (Not the Problem)**

    Make sure guidance is specific, actionable, and tells people what to do. Find ways to abbreviate frequently-given solutions to make them easier and faster to apply.

30. **Lock It In**

    To insure feedback is fully received as intended, ask recipients to summarize it, prioritize important parts, and identify their first step in implementation.

31. **Normalize Error**

    People will not take risks if they are afraid to fail. Approach error as an opportunity to learn.

32. **Break Down the Barriers to Practice**

    Practice can be stressful and sometimes scary. Develop strategies for overcoming barriers in order to start practicing successfully.

33. **Make It Fun to Practice**

    Integrate elements of play, competition, and surprise to cultivate an environment where practice is both valued and enjoyed.

34. **Everybody Does It**

    In a true culture of learning, top leadership can't just stand back and watch. Model risk taking and openness to feedback in order to invest others in practice.

35. **Leverage Peer-to-Peer Accountability**

    When people on teams make mutual commitments to each other, investment and follow through are more likely to occur.

36. **Hire for Practice**

    Build a team that is open and ready to do the hard work of practice. Ask candidates to practice and implement your feedback.

37. **Praise the Work**

    Normalize praise that is meaningful and supports the work your team is doing. Praise actions, not traits. Differentiate acknowledgment from praise.

38. **Look for the Right Things**

    Closely align what you look for in performance with skills taught in practice. Create observation tools to keep a focus on the right things.

39. **Coach During the Game (Don't Teach)**

    Performance is a time for cues and reminders. Introducing new skills should be reserved for practice.

40. **Keep Talking**

    Take the shared vocabulary developed during practice into the field. Finesse it to create a shorthand for communicating (but not teaching!) during performance and when debriefing.

41. **Walk the Line (Between Support and Demand)**

    Be the warm/strict coach. Reward hard work *and* communicate urgency when improvement is necessary.

42. **Measure Success**

    Measurement drives results. Gather data during performance to improve practice.

INDEX